YOU SEE, WHAT REALLY HAPPENED IS...
AND OTHER PLAYS

By

Craig Christie

FOR ALL ENQUIRIES CONTACT: ORiGiN™ Theatrical
PO BOX Q1235, QVB Post Office, Sydney, NSW, 1230, Australia
Phone: (61 2) 8514 5201 Fax: (61 2) 9299 2920
enquiries@originmusic.com.au   www.origintheatrical.com.au
Part of the ORiGiN™ Music Group
An Australian Independent Music Company

IMPORTANT NOTICE

First Published © 2018 ORiGiN™ Theatrical

The amateur and professional acting rights to this work are controlled exclusively by ORiGiN™ Theatrical (the publisher). Permission in writing is required by ORiGiN™ Theatrical, or their agent, before a performance is given. A performance is given any time it is acted before an audience. A royalty fee is payable before each and every performance regardless of whether it is for a non-profit organisation or if an admission is charged.

The publication of this play does not mean that the amateur and professional performance rights are available. It is highly recommended that you apply for performance rights before starting rehearsals and/or booking rehearsal or performance spaces.

Visit the ORiGiN™ Theatrical website for applications and information www.origintheatrical.com.au or address your inquiry to ORiGiN™ Theatrical, PO Box Q1235, QVB Post Office, Sydney, NSW 1230, Australia.

This work is fully protected by copyright. No alterations, substitutions or deletions can be made to this work without the prior consent of the publisher. It is expressly prohibited to broadcast, televise, film, videotape, record, translate or transmit to subscribers through a diffusion service that currently exists or is yet to be invented, this work or any portion thereof whatsoever without permission in writing from the publisher.

Copying or reproducing, without permission, of all or any part of this book, in any form, is an infringement of copyright.

Copyright provides the creators with an incentive to invest their time, talent and other resources to create new works. Authors earn their living from the royalties they receive from book sales and from the performance of the work. Copyright law provides a legal framework for control of their creations.

Whenever this play is produced, the billing and credit requirements *must* appear on all programs distributed in connection with the performance and in all instances in which the title of the play appears for the purposes of advertising, seeking publicity for the play or otherwise exploiting the play and/or a performance(s).

While this play may contain references to brand names or trademarks owned by third parties, or make reference to public figures, ORiGiN™ Theatrical should not be considered to be necessarily endorsing or otherwise attempting to promote an affiliation with any of the owners of the brand names or trademarks or public figures. Such references are solely for use in a dramatic context.

If you are in any doubt about any of the above then contact ORiGiN™ Theatrical.

LANGUAGE NOTE

Licensees are welcome to make small alterations to the language that is used is this play so as to make it suitable for a younger cast and/or audience.

www.origintheatrical.com.au

AND HERE ARE THE RULES IN PLAIN ENGLISH FOR YOU...

DO NOT perform this play without getting permission from ORiGiN™ Theatrical first. In 99% of cases you'll need to pay us money to be allowed to stage a performance. This money goes to the author(s) of the show who shed blood, sweat and tears creating this play. Please don't rob them of their livelihood.
Go online www.origintheatrical.com.au or call +61 2 8514 5201

DO NOT make a copy of this book by photocopying, scanning, taking a photo, retyping (on a computer or a typewriter), or using a pencil, pen or chalkboard. If you want to purchase more copies contact ORiGiN™ Theatrical.
Go online www.origintheatrical.com.au or call +61 2 8514 5201

DO NOT make any changes to the text without first getting permission from ORiGiN™ Theatrical in writing. Sometimes you'll be allowed to make changes and sometimes you won't. Please always check with us first.
Go online www.origintheatrical.com.au or call +61 2 8514 5201

DO NOT record your performances or rehearsals in anyway without first getting permission from ORiGiN™ Theatrical. We know everyone wants to try and record everything on their phones these days. We get it. But please don't encourage them or give them permission. Sometimes there are important contractual reasons as to why we can't give you permission to record it. And sometimes there aren't any reasons and we can say YES. Please just check with us first.
Go online www.origintheatrical.com.au or call +61 2 8514 5201

DO contact ORiGiN™ Theatrical if you have any questions about anything. At all. And we mean anything. One of us that works here (not me) has a peculiar interest in recording the unusual bird calls of the adult hoatzin (a species of tropical bird found in wet forest and mangrove of the Amazon and the Orinoco delta in South America) so we should be able to answer any questions you have about the Hoatzin. Plus we know some things about some other things too.

Thank you for taking the time to read this.

BY THE SAME AUTHOR

Connected

Jungle Bungle

Rev It Up!

Eurobeat: Moldova

Craig Christie Songbook

The Web, Wires & Waves

INTRODUCTION

This collection of short plays was selected from a large number of scripts that were developed with secondary school students in schools throughout the Mallee region of North-Western Victoria during my tenure as Artistic Development Coordinator for the George Fairfax Memorial Arts Festival from between 1998 and 2005. During this time I drove over 40,000 km visiting schools in often remote settings to work with groups of students to help them create a short performance piece for the festival which was held annually in the town of Swan Hill (and occasionally Mildura). This festival brought together students from remote settings to share and enjoy the work of their peers in a celebration of fellowship and creativity. The students would set the agenda of these performances and I variously workshopped, wrote, directed or acted as a consultant for over 100 pieces during this time. The range of topics and styles reflects the particular nature of each of the groups I worked with – some exploring issues of identity, some reflecting popular culture and some just for fun.

One never knows where the impression made by being able to participate in the arts and share the experience with others may lead. Certainly for students in remote rural areas without access to theatres or even qualified staff and facilities within their school the chance to work with theatre professionals and see the work of their peers the affect can be profound. One of my favourite stories from this time is about the young boy living in the small and remote town of Sea Lake who participated in my first Festival in 1998. As a result of that experience he pursued a career in the theatre that has lead to him being one of the most in demand stage managers on London's West End!

As these pieces were created to be able to be performed with a minimum amount of technical support the focus is on what the performers can bring to script. There is a minimum of stage direction and character outlines which hopefully will encourage any group to bring their own interpretations to the fore. In keeping with the original intention of the writing of these scripts in whatever context they may now be utilised the emphasis should continue to be about participation, creativity and enjoyment for all participants.

Craig Christie

For more information on Craig Christie visit
www.nomatesproductions.com

CONTENTS

- YOU SEE, WHAT REALLY HAPPENED IS............................11
- ICE 27
- LOSING MY PATIENTS...43
- ONE NIGHT… 59
- SNOW WHITE AND THE SEVEN SINS 77
- HUSH..97
- FIFTEEN MINUTES OF FAME..109
- THE GREAT PRETENDER 127
- CHRISTMAS TURKEY..141

<u>YOU SEE, WHAT REALLY HAPPENED IS...</u>

CHARACTERS
CHARLIE
SYLVIA
SCARLETT
NED
MS. NIXON
CHANTELLE

The basic setting is four chairs in a semi circle with Ms. Nixon pacing around. The characters move into the centre space to act out their stories then return to their seats.
Everyone who is not involved in the action remains frozen.

SPECIAL NOTE: The character of Chantelle was created for a cast member who was profoundly hearing impaired and unable to speak.

CHARLIE, SYLVIA, SCARLETT AND NED ARE ALL SITTING ON CHAIRS LOOKING UNCOMFORTABLE AND ANXIOUS.
MS. NIXON IS PACING AROUND THE ROOM, HOLDING ONTO A CLIPBOARD. EVENTUALLY THE SILENCE BECOMES TOO MUCH.

MS. NIXON: Well we all know what we're here for. Someone must have something to say. NO REPLY. Come on now. You're wasting my time and your own. Who is going first?

NED: I got nothin' to say.

SCARLETT: You never have anything to say.

SYLVIA: At least he's not like you. You never shut up.

SCARLETT: Look who's talking.

CHARLIE: Don't start you two.

SCARLETT: She started it.

CHARLIE: Just shut up both of you. You've got nothing to worry about. I'm going to talk.

MS. NIXON: What do you mean Charlie?

CHARLIE: Like I said. I'm going to talk.

SYLVIA: Be careful. She's writing everything down.

CHARLIE: Yeah, yeah. I know. Anything I say may be held in evidence against me in a court of law. I know the drill. I've heard it a thousand times before.

MS: NIXON: What did you want to say Charlie?

CHARLIE: Look I know why you've brought us all here. The real reason. No need to try and pretend it's for anything else. I guess I've had enough of all the messing around. There's something I want to tell you all about the 13th of August.

SYLVIA: Be careful Charlie. You don't have to do this.

SCARLETT: You don't have to say anything. Sometimes it's better to keep your mouth shut.

CHARLIE: No I want to talk. There's no need in keeping all the others in here. I'm the one you want. The others can all go home.

MS. NIXON: What do you mean Charlie.

CHARLIE: I was there on 13th August. I saw it all. You see, what really happened is I was doing overtime that night and I'd been called in to the hotel to look at a bit of faulty wiring. The hotel was old and I was often called in to check out the electrics. Well when I arrived she was there waiting for me. I can see it all so clearly, as if it was happening right now.
HE GETS UP FROM HIS SEAT, GRABS HIS TOOL BOX AND COMES FORWARD. CHANTELLE, THE MAID, COMES OUT.

CHARLIE: Hello Chantelle. Problems with the wiring I hear. Where do I need to go this time? CHANTELLE POINTS THE DIRECTION. Oh how about you show me what is wrong? It will save a lot of time. SHE SHRUGS AND LEADS HIM TO A ROOM AND POINTS TO A POWER SOCKET.

CHARLIE: All right. I'll get to work. HE GETS OUT A SCREWDRIVER AND STARTS TO FIDDLE WITH THE POWER POINT. Chantelle. Could you please go and make sure that the power is turned off. I don't want to electrocute myself. This can be dangerous work. SHE EXITS. It's difficult working with her watching me. Sometimes I think that she suspects that it was I who was responsible for her Grandmother's death. But it was all a terrible accident. How was I to know that the old bag was going to try and turn on her hairdryer just as I was connecting the power? It was a terrible shame that the power surge fried the old woman's brains completely but it wasn't my fault. Besides no-one knows I was there at all that day.

If only she wouldn't look at me with those sad, suspicious eyes. Oh well I'd best get the job done and then get away from here. HE STARTS FIDDLING WITH THE POWER POINT WITH HIS SCREWDRIVER THEN IS KNOCKED BACKWARDS AS IF RECEIVING A TERRIBLE SHOCK. CHANTELLE COMES IN TO SEE HIM LYING ON HIS BACK. WHEN SHE GETS CLOSER HE JUMPS UP.

CHARLIE: Ah ha. You thought you had me then didn't you Chantelle. You tried to kill me by turning on the electricity but you weren't counting on me wearing my special rubber soled boots to insulate me against electric shocks. You little fool. You can't kill me off that easily. So you do know about me and your Grandmother, don't you? SHE NODS, TERRIFIED. Well I'll make sure that you never tell anyone else.
HE RUNS FORWARD AND STABS HER WITH HIS SCREWDRIVER. WHEN SHE FALLS HE DRAGS HER OFFSTAGE, COMES BACK AND TAKES HIS SEAT.

CHARLIE: And that is what really happened.

MS. NIXON: Are you sure that is what happened? You don't want to add anything else to your story?

CHARLIE: No that's the truth. I've confessed it so you may as well let the others go.

SYLVIA: No Charlie. You don't have to tell them this story.

CHARLIE: It's all right Sylvia. I feel better now that I've told the truth and got it off my chest.

SYLVIA: But it's not the truth. You know it. Tell her the real story Charlie.

MS. NIXON: What is the real story Sylvia?

SYLVIA: You see what really happened is on that night I was at home watching to see when Charlie got home. You see he lives down the road and sometimes I pop over for pizza and Netflix on a Friday night. Well I waited and waited because he usually gets home at about 5.30 and by 5.45 I decided that he must have had a work call. I decided to go into town to pick up the pizza for when he finally got home. I know he loves Hawaiian. When I got there I noticed Charlie's car out the front of the hotel so I went in.
IN THE HOTEL. CHANTELLE IS THERE.

SYLVIA: Chantelle. Have you seen Charlie anywhere?
SHE POINTS DOWN THE HALL. SYLVIA FINDS CHARLIE AT WORK AT THE ELECTRIC SWITCH.

SYLVIA: Charlie. What are you doing?

CHARLIE: Hello Sylvia. Sorry about pizza but I had a late call.

SYLVIA: A late call eh. A likely story.

CHARLIE: What do you mean? I was called here to fix the electric switch in this room.

SYLVIA: Called here by whom? It was Chantelle, I bet.

CHARLIE: Chantelle? What do you mean?

SYLVIA: I have long suspected that you and Chantelle have a relationship that is more than simply professional. Those nights that you come home late. Don't try to tell me now that you have been out working. I know that you have been here with her.

CHARLIE: And what if I have been here with her. What business is it of yours?

SYLVIA: Oh you heartless man. Don't you see. I have been waiting for you to notice me for all these years, hanging out for those nights of pizza and watching Netflix with me, hoping that some romance may come about.

CHARLIE: But Sylvia. I thought we were just friends.

SYLVIA: But I want to be so much more. But how can that ever happen when you keep on rushing after Chantelle all of the time.

CHARLIE: No. You've got it all wrong.

SYLVIA: Have I? We'll see about that. CALLS OUT. Chantelle. Come here.

CHARLIE: What are you doing?

SYLVIA: I'm going to settle this one and for all. CALLING. Chantelle. Come here now! CHANTELLE ENTERS. Now I want you to tell me - are you having a secret affair with Charlie? No, there's no need to say a word. I can see it in your eyes. You are in love with him.

CHARLIE: You're imagining it Sylvia. It is you that I love.

SYLVIA: Oh it's all very well to say that now I have caught you out.

CHARLIE: No it's true. I have treasured those Friday nights with you eating pizza and watching Netflix. You have always been my one true love. I just never knew how to tell you.

SYLVIA: Liar. I know that she has stolen your heart. But I won't let her get away with it. SHE PULLS OUT HER NAIL FILE.

CHARLIE: What are you going to do with that nail file? Sylvia, control yourself.

SYLVIA: Control myself. Where is your self control? Where is hers? I am putting an end to this once and for all. SHE STABS CHANTELLE WITH HER NAIL FILE. CHANTELLE COLLAPSES TO THE FLOOR. Oh dear. I have been rather hasty. What I have I done?

CHARLIE: CHECKING. She's dead. Oh Sylvia. What are we going to do now?

SYLVIA: I'm sorry Charlie. I don't know what came over me.

CHARLIE: We'll have to hide the body. Come on. HE DRAGS THE BODY OUT.

SYLVIA: And that's what really happened. It was me. A crime of passion. I don't know what came over me but you have to see now it was me that murdered Chantelle. Don't listen to Charlie. He is just trying to cover up for me.

MS. NIXON: What do you have to say about that Charlie?

CHARLIE: Don't believe her. She is just trying to take the blame for something that I did. But it was me.

SYLVIA: No. Me.

CHARLIE: Me.

SYLVIA: Me.

SCARLETT: Enough. Be quiet both of you. You don't need to cover up anything anymore. It's time we let her know, let her know the truth.

NED: Oh here we go.

CHARLIE: What are you talking about?

SYLVIA: I don't understand.

SCARLETT: It's no use. They're going to work out together all the pieces of the puzzle in the end. I did it. I killed Chantelle.

MS. NIXON: Would you like to tell me about it Scarlett?

SCARLETT: You see what really happened is I had checked into the hotel where everything happened the night of the murder. I knew that Chantelle had been working there for a while. In fact I knew more than anyone could suspect. You see, I am Chantelle's sister. And I knew exactly what she was up to. SCARLETT ENTERS THE HOTEL. SHE CALLS.

SCARLETT: Chantelle. CHANTELLE ENTERS. There you are. I thought that you'd be surprised to see me. Yes you thought that you'd managed to hide yourself away but you couldn't hide forever. Don't bother saying anything. I'm not interested in hearing any more of your lies. You can talk later once I have had a chance to catch up with my lawyers. CHARLIE ENTERS.

CHARLIE: Hello Chantelle. Trouble with the electricity again is it? How about you show me where the problem is.

CHANTELLE LEADS CHARLIE OUT OF THE ROOM. SYLVIA ENTERS.

SYLVIA: Scarlett. What are you doing here? I thought you were away overseas.

SCARLETT: That's what I wanted everyone to think. It gave me time to take care of some unfinished business.

SYLVIA: What are you talking about?

SCARLETT: It's Chantelle. You might know her as the maid here at the hotel but there are many dim, dark secrets in her past.

SYLVIA: There aren't just secrets in her past. I reckon she's up to something with Charlie, the electrician from down the road who I have secretly been in love with for years.

SCARLETT: That doesn't surprise me. People think that she is so sweet and quiet but I know that inside she is rotten to the core.

SYLVIA: What do you mean?

SCARLETT: It all began when Grandfather died suddenly. No-one suspected anything at first because he was old and frail anyway, so it wasn't surprising that he would trip and fall down the stairs, breaking his neck. After Grandfather died, people weren't surprised that Grandmother followed soon after, although I thought it was odd that she should electrocute herself in such a peculiar way while drying her hair. It was even possibly only just a coincidence when the brake cable broke in the Mercedes when Mother and Father were coming home from Grandmother's funeral and they drove right off the side of the cliff. However, when our brother died supposedly from belting himself in the head with a hammer I began to think that there was too much going on for it all to be just chance.

SYLVIA: What do you mean Scarlett?

SCARLETT: I suspect that Chantelle has been murdering all of our relatives so that she can inherit the family fortune. Now there is only her and me.

SYLVIA: Then what is she doing here then, working as a maid if she is in line for a fortune.

SCARLETT: After our brother's funeral the police started to ask a few questions. I think that Chantelle left home to try and keep out of their way for a while until the police finished their investigations. But I have followed her here to try and get her to confess to her crimes.

SYLVIA: But if she really is a cunning killer then Charlie may not be safe at all. We must go and help him. THEY GO INTO A ROOM TO FIND CHARLIE WORKING ON A POWER POINT WHEN HE SUDDENLY IS THROWN BACKWARDS BY A POWER SURGE. SYLVIA RUNS FORWARD.

SYLVIA: Charlie. Are you all right? SCARLETT FOLLOWS CLOSE BEHIND.

CHARLIE: I'm fine, I think. Who turned the power back on?

SCARLETT: We all know the answer to that. There's no use in hiding Chantelle. You can come out now. CHANTELLE ENTERS. The game is up. I have here a document for you to sign admitting your guilt in the murder of our family so you could get your hands on the inheritance. HOLDING OUT A PEN. Come over here and sign it now. CHANTELLE MOVES

TOWARDS SCARLETT SLOWLY THEN SUDDENLY PULLS OUT A GUN.

SYLVIA: Watch out Scarlett.

CHARLIE: She's armed and dangerous.

SCARLETT: Put it away Chantelle. You're only making things worse for yourself. CHARLIE MAKES A GRAB FOR THE GUN. CHANTELLE DROPS IT AND RUNS TOWARDS SCARLETT WHO STABS HER WITH THE PEN.

SYLVIA: What have you done?

SCARLETT: It was revenge for our family. She's paid the price for her wicked ways.

CHARLIE: But you killed her.

SCARLETT: I can always say it was self defence.

SYLVIA: But don't you see. With her dead without signing the confession everyone is bound to think that it was you who did away with the family to get the inheritance.

SCARLETT: Oh you've got to help me. What am I going to do?

CHARLIE: Look I'll hide the body. With a bit of luck we can all be far away before they find the body. HE DRAGS THE BODY OFF.

SYLVIA: Let's go. We don't want to get caught hanging around here.

SCARLETT: And that's what really happened

MS. NIXON: Is there anything else you'd like to add to this story Scarlett?

SCARLETT: Only that it really was me that did it and that Chantelle deserved it.

SYLVIA: This is just ridiculous. Surely it's obvious that I'm the guilty one.

CHARLIE: Don't listen to them. It was me.

SCARLETT: There's no need to cover up for me. I'm ready to pay for my crime.

SYLVIA: It's not your crime.

CHARLIE: It's my crime.

MS. NIXON: Ned. Have you got anything to add to this?

NED: Nope.

MS. NIXON: Are you sure? Everyone else has had their say.

NED: Well I've got nothing to add. I don't even know why you've brought me here with them. I shouldn't be here in the first place.

MS. NIXON: Well why do you think we have brought you here then Ned?

NED: I don't know. You might have been able to get a confession out of the others but you'll get nothing from me.

MS. NIXON: You sound like you're hiding something.

NED: Look I might have something to say but I just don't see the point when no-one will believe me.

MS. NIXON: What do you mean?

NED: Well you see, if you want to know what went on the night of the 13th of August there's no point in asking them. They don't really know.

SCARLETT: Liar!

SYLVIA: We do so know what went on.

CHARLIE: We were there. I don't remember seeing you anywhere near the hotel that night.

NED: I'm not surprised. But I was there. You see, what really happened is I was waiting in the bar of the hotel for a drink. There was no-one serving and I got sick of waiting so I went looking for someone to get me a beer. I walked into a room just in time to see something strange.
SCARLETT, SYLVIA AND CHARLIE ARE ALL STANDING IN THE ROOM. CHANTELLE IS POINTING A STRANGE GUN AT THEM.

CHARLIE: I knew we should have called the Men in Black earlier.

SCARLETT: Now this alien has us in her power and there is nothing we can do about it.

SYLVIA: We've tracked her half way around the world only to be caught.

CHARLIE: If she fires that special mind gun at us, we'll forget everything that happened. Our minds will be blank and she'll be able to program any memories she wants. We won't remember what happened - only what she wants us to think.

SCARLETT: We're going to have to try and jump her.

SYLVIA: Are you ready? On my signal. Now! THEY JUMP FOR CHANTELLE BUT SHE FIRES THE RAY GUN AT THEM AND THEY FALL DOWN UNCONCSCIOUS.

NED: I don't know what you've done to them but you're not going to get away with it. Watch out. I'm armed. I have a fork here. CHANTELLE LUNGES AT NED WHO STABS HER WITH A FORK. SHE COLLAPSES. Now what am I going to do? Those people will be no help. They will have different memories planted in their brains by now. I'll just have to get rid of the body and hope for the best. HE DRAGS THE BODY OUT. THE OTHERS GET UP SLOWLY AND TAKE THEIR SEATS. NED COMES BACK IN.

NED: And that's what really happened. THERE IS SILENCE FOR A MOMENT.

CHARLIE: Well that is one of the most stupid stories that I have ever heard.

SYLVIA: Surely you're not going to listen to that pile of rubbish?

SCARLETT: He obviously watches too much television.

NED: Of course that's what you think. You've had your brains scrambled.

CHARLIE: There's only one person in here with scrambled brains mate.

MS. NIXON: There's no need for that. Look I don't think we're going to get any further with our session today. It's probably time for your medication anyway everyone. CALLS. Nurse. We're going to finish the session now. ENTER CHANTELLE. Thankyou nurse. You can show the patients back to their wards now. I'm afraid we don't seem to be making much progress at the moment. We'll see you all next week.

CHARLIE: Hello Chantelle. Is it time for our medicine now?

SYLVIA: I don't really want to go back just yet. Can we stay out for a bit longer?

SCARLETT: We'll tell you a story.

NED: If we tell you a story will you let us go to bed without restraints tonight?

CHARLIE: Did I tell you how I murdered the Doctor last week.

SYLVIA: No you didn't. It was me. I killed her.

SCARLETT: There's no need to cover up on my behalf. I'm the one who killed Doctor Nixon.

NED: Dr. Nixon is an alien. Didn't you know?

TOGETHER: You see, what really happened is....

THE END

ICE

CHARACTERS
COURTNEY
BOB
Courtney's Friends
BESSY
JILL
PATSY
HARRIET
The Authority Figures
TEACHER
MOTHER
FATHER
PRIEST

TEACHER FIGURE STANDS CALLS 'ENTER'. THE CAST ASSEMBLES WALKING IN SINGLE FILE, ROBOT LIKE. TEACHER SAYS 'TURN'. THEY DO. TEACHER SAYS 'GOOD MORNING'. CAST RESPONDS. TEACHER SAYS SIT. THEY DO.

TEACHER: Right class. Today is the day that I want you to give your talks on what you want to be when you grow up. Come forward when I call you and speak in a clear loud voice. POINTING AT BESSY You! Come forward. BESSY COMES FORWARD.

BESSY: When I grow up I want to be a nurse. Mother and Father say that is a good career as I will be able to care for people. I must study hard as I need a good education to take a useful place in society. People like and respect nurses so that is what I am going to be.

TEACHER: POINTS AT JILL. Come forward.

JILL: I would like to work in law enforcement when I grow up. I will make people understand that if you are obedient and understand what is expected of you as a citizen you can have a place for yourself in society.

TEACHER: POINTS AT PATSY. Come forward.

PATSY: When I grow up I want to be a teacher. I will study hard to get a good education and then go to college to learn how to teach children to be obedient and cooperative. I want a career where people will do as I say without asking questions so I want to be a good teacher like you Mr. Frost. Mother and Father say that teaching is a useful career so they will be pleased if that is what I become.

TEACHER: POINTS AT COURTNEY. Come forward.

COURTNEY: Mr. Frost, girls and boys. I haven't quite decided what I want to do when I grow up yet because there are so many different things I want to try. I want to be a famous dancer and travel the world and then maybe be an explorer and swing with the monkeys in the Amazon rain forest and then go riding across the Sahara on my camel.
Of course I could be a writer and make up really interesting stories or maybe be an actor and...

TEACHER: Enough. Be quiet.

COURTNEY: But there is so much more.

TEACHER: I said be quiet. Go and stand in the corner and stay there until you can think of a sensible answer.

COURTNEY: But I would like to be a dancer.

TEACHER: Go! COURTNEY GOES TO THE CORNER. Pay no attention to her class. She is a foolish girl. Now I would like you to write out five pages from an employment website for homework. That will teach you the value of a job. Class dismissed. THE CLASS FILES OUT. THE TEACHER LEAVES, LEAVING COURTNEY ALONE IN THE CORNER. MOTHER AND FATHER ENTER AND STAND, LOOKING DOWN ON COURTNEY.

FATHER: Courtney, come here.

COURTNEY: Yes Daddy.

FATHER: We had a message from your school again Courtney. They say you have been acting up again.

COURTNEY: I haven't done anything wrong.

FATHER: Your teacher says that you have been wasting your time again daydreaming.

COURTNEY: I do all my school work.

FATHER: That is not the point. You spend too much time dreaming about things Courtney and not enough time in the real world.

MOTHER: Father is only thinking of you Courtney. Mr Frost is looking out for your best interests as well. This isn't the old days when school didn't help you make choices. Now they are there to help you find good and useful positions. Remember the world is a competitive place and you need to make use of every opportunity.

FATHER: You need to be thinking about your future now, not wasting time with silly dreams. The world is a hard place Courtney.

MOTHER: And a cold place Courtney.

FATHER: And dreams don't keep you warm at night and put food in your stomach.

COURTNEY: That's where you're wrong. My dreams can keep me warm.

FATHER: Where does she get these stupid ideas Mother?

MOTHER: I don't know Father.

FATHER: Perhaps she is reading too many books. They can be dangerous. Fill a girl's head with all manner of silly ideas. Courtney, you are to stop reading so many books and spend your time more usefully. Perhaps if you spent more time at the computer you would have a better idea of what the world is about.

COURTNEY: Yes Daddy.

MOTHER: Now go and set the table for dinner Courtney. It's five to six. We need to be ready for dinner in five minutes.

FATHER: Don't want to mess with our routine.

COURTNEY: I'll do it now Mummy. SHE GOES TO HUG HER MOTHER.

MOTHER: Good heavens girl. What do you think you are doing?

COURTNEY: I just wanted to give you a hug.

MOTHER: Oh you're too old for that kind of nonsense. Just go and set the table like we asked you. COURTNEY LEAVES

FATHER: She's a problem, that girl.

MOTHER: Perhaps she needs some other interests to give her a bit more direction.

FATHER: A pity she's too young to join the Army Reserve. That sort of discipline would be good for her.

MOTHER: Perhaps we could get more involved in the church. She could join one of the youth groups, teach Sunday School maybe. Something nice. Something useful.

FATHER: Perhaps.

MOTHER: Well a lot of her friends are involved. I'll speak to Father Zero about it.

FATHER: It can't do any harm. THEY LEAVE. FATHER ZERO ENTERS TO TAKE THEIR PLACE. THE CONGREGATION ENTERS IN A SIMILAR FASHION TO THE SCHOOL AT THE BEGINNING.

PRIEST: Obedience. Respect. Humility. Thou shalt. Thou shalt not. Thou shalt. Thou shalt not. Thou shalt. Thou shalt not. Amen. THE CONGREGATION LEAVES EXCEPT FOR COURTNEY WHO GOES UP TO THE PRIEST.

COURTNEY: Good morning Father Zero.

PRIEST: Courtney. How are you?

COURTNEY: I'm fine thank you.

PRIEST: What can I do for you?

COURTNEY: My parents said I should have a talk with you.

PRIEST: Ah yes, that's right. And how are they?

COURTNEY: They're fine.

PRIEST: Courtney, your parents are concerned that your life lacks a bit of direction at the moment.

COURTNEY: I don't know why Father Zero. I'm getting good marks at school. I'm not causing any trouble at all at home.

PRIEST: Of course not. We all know you are a good girl.

COURTNEY: If this is about me deciding what to do with my future then they shouldn't worry. I'm sure I'm going to get good enough marks to get into the course I want to.

PRIEST: And what course is that?

COURTNEY: Performing Arts. I want to study to be an actress.

PRIEST: But Courtney, surely you know that that is not a real career. You can't make a living as an actress. And it is a dangerous choice for a young woman. There are all kinds of moral dangers in that world. You are a bright girl. It's such a waste of your intelligence. You could study teaching perhaps or get into accounting or law. Something your parents could be proud of.

COURTNEY: My parents should be proud of me whatever I choose to do.

PRIEST: You should honour thy Father and thy Mother Courtney.

COURTNEY: But who is going to honour me? Father Zero I don't want to be disrespectful but what about my happiness.

PRIEST: You should be happy being a good and dutiful girl.

COURTNEY: But I am a good girl. If I go off to study acting it's no different to taking any other course. I'm not stupid or naive. I know if there are bad things going on to keep away from them.

PRIEST: The road to hell is paved with good intentions.

COURTNEY: Yes Father Zero.

PRIEST: Go now Courtney. Just think about what I have said.

COURTNEY: Yes Father Zero.

PRIEST: That's a good girl. God bless. HE EXITS. COURTNEY'S FRIENDS ENTER.

BESSY: Hi Courtney.

JILL: Hi Courtney.

PATSY: Hi Courtney.

HARRIET: Hi Courtney.

TOGETHER: What's happening?

COURTNEY: Oh nothing much really. Just studying as usual.

BESSY: How is university?

JILL: What's accounting like?

PATSY: Lots of work?

HARRIET: Any cute boys? THEY ALL GIGGLE TOGETHER.

COURTNEY: It's alright I suppose.

BESSY: Have you heard about Sally Mumford?

JILL: She just got engaged.

PATSY: To Peter, Mr. Frost's son.

HARRIET: Fancy having our old primary school teacher as a father-in-law.

TOGETHER: How hilarious.

COURTNEY: No I hadn't heard.

BESSY: Well the engagement party is next weekend.

JILL: We're all going.

PATSY: You have to come.

HARRIET: It will be great fun.

COURTNEY: I'd love to go.

BESSY: What will we wear?

JILL: I don't know. What are you wearing?

PATSY: I don't know. What are you wearing?

HARRIET: I don't know. What are you wearing?

COURTNEY: I bought this great new dress in town. It's really fitted. It's red. Looks great.

ALL: Oh Courtney.

BESSY: You can't wear something like that.

JILL: How could you think of that?

PATSY: Everyone will look at you?

HARRIET: Everyone will talk about you?

ALL: It wouldn't be right.

COURTNEY: But I like it. I think it looks good.

ALL: Let's all wear our white dresses.

BESSY: You must have a white dress Courtney.

JILL: Why don't you wear it?

PATSY: We could all go together.

HARRIET: We could all look the same.

ALL: It'll be cool.

COURTNEY: I'll think about it.

ALL: See you there. THEY EXIT.

COURTNEY: Where do I go from here?

THE AUTHORITY FIGURES - TEACHER, MOTHER, FATHER AND PRIEST - ENTER AND STAND ON BLOCKS ACROSS THE BACK OF THE STAGE. THE FRIENDS ENTER IN A LINE. AS EACH FRIEND SPEAKS THEY ATTACH A LINE FROM THE TALLER FIGURES TO COURTNEY'S WRISTS AND ANKLES.

TEACHER: Go and stand in the corner until you can think of a sensible answer.

BESSY: I wonder where Courtney was on Saturday night

FATHER: You spend too much time dreaming about things and not enough time in the real world.

JILL: Haven't you heard? She's in hospital.

MOTHER: You're too old for that kind of nonsense.

PATSY: Did she have an accident?

PRIEST: The road to hell is paved with good intentions.

HARRIET: No. She's had a nervous breakdown. THE TALL FIGURES PULL THE STRINGS AND COURTNEY IS LIKE A PUPPET.

TEACHER: Get your head out of the clouds.

MOTHER: Be a good girl.

FATHER: Don't waste your time on dreams.

PRIEST: Do the right thing. ENTER BOB.

BOB: Hello.

COURTNEY: Hello.

BOB: I'm Bob.

COURTNEY: I'm Courtney.

BOB: How long have you been here?

COURTNEY: I don't know.

BOB: I'm not sure how long I've been here either.

COURTNEY: Why were you put in here?

BOB: Because life presented me with too many choices. Why were you put in here.

COURTNEY: Because life didn't present me with enough. Could I hold your hand for a moment.

BOB: Why?

COURTNEY: So I know that I am real.

BOB: All right. HE REACHES OUT AND TOUCHES HER HAND AND THE FIGURES RELEASE THE STRINGS. Here let me help you. HE TAKES THE STRINGS FROM HER. Would you like to go for a walk? THEY EXIT TOGETHER.

MOTHER: Isn't it wonderful.

FATHER: Who would have thought.

MOTHER: She seems so much more settled.

FATHER: Happier than I've seen her in years.

MOTHER: And Bob is such a nice boy.

FATHER: So sensible.

MOTHER: So stable.

FATHER: Our little girl seems on the right track at last.

PRIEST: God moves in mysterious ways. THEY EXIT. ENTER BOB AND COURTNEY.

BOB: I can't believe how good things are now. Six months ago I thought that everything was lost. Now I've got a great job. I've got you. Everything seems so clear and straightforward now.

COURTNEY: For you maybe. I'm still not sure. Since I dropped that horrible course at uni I still haven't figured out what I want.

BOB: Give yourself time. There's no rush.

COURTNEY: Well there is one thing.

BOB: What's that?

COURTNEY: When I was younger I always dreamed about being a dancer. Well I know it's a bit late to start that but I also wanted to study acting. Maybe I could try to get into a drama course. It's something I always wanted to do but no-one ever seemed to like the idea.

BOB: Why would you want to do that? Acting's not a real job.

COURTNEY: Why does everyone talk about real jobs all the time? Maybe some things you should do just because you want to. Just because if you don't do them you'll never know and spend your whole life thinking 'what if'.

BOB: Well I have something else to say that if I don't I'll always wonder 'what if'.

COURTNEY: What's that?

BOB: Courtney, will you marry me?

COURTNEY: What?

BOB: If we get married then we'll both be secure. You'll be able to do anything you want then.

COURTNEY: Are you sure?

BOB: Trust me.

COURTNEY: I always thought that there'd be flowers and music and a guy on one knee begging for my hand in marriage. I never expected to be proposed to like this.

BOB: This is life, not the movies.

COURTNEY: When you put it that way...

BOB: Don't be like that.

COURTNEY: Do you love me?

BOB: What sort of a question is that?

COURTNEY: Well do you?

BOB: I'm prepared to spend the rest of my life with you, care for you, make you safe. Doesn't that answer your question.

COURTNEY: No. Not really.

BOB: Look I don't know what you're hoping for Courtney but I reckon that this is as good as it gets. Don't mess around with our future.

COURTNEY: As good as it gets.

BOB: Will you marry me?

COURTNEY: Yes Bob. I will marry you. THEY EXIT. THE AUTHORITY FIGURES ENTER.

MOTHER: I'm so happy.

FATHER: Our little girl is finally going to be settled.

MOTHER: And he's such a nice boy.

FATHER: So sensible. BOB ENTERS AND STANDS AT THE PRIEST'S FEET. COURTNEY ENTERS AS A BRIDE WITH HER FOUR FRIENDS AS BRIDESMAIDS. THE BRIDESMAID'S ATTACH THE STRINGS FROM THE FIGURES TO COURTNEY'S HANDS AND FEET. THEY MOVE HER LIKE A PUPPET TO BOB'S SIDE.

PRIEST: Dearly beloved. We are gathered here today...

COURTNEY: It's so cold.

PRIEST: To join this man and this woman...

COURTNEY: Everything is so cold.

PRIEST: Do you Courtney take this man...

COURTNEY: Why do I feel so cold?

PRIEST: Do you promise to love, honour and obey. ON EACH WORD BOB TAKES THE LINE FROM COURTNEY'S FEET AND HANDS AND PUTS THEM AROUND HER NECK.

PRIEST: Do you Bob...

BOB: I do.

PRIEST: Courtney?

EVERYONE: She does.

COURTNEY: I do. THE FIGURES PULL THE STRINGS, STRANGLING HER. SHE FALLS TO THE GROUND. BOB PICKS HER UP.

BOB: She's so cold.

COURTNEY TURNS AROUND AND HER FACE IS A WHITE MASK.

THE END

LOSING MY PATIENTS

CHARACTERS
NURSE TILLY
NURSE TANSY
NURSE NANCY – a sweet new nurse
MATRON – overbearing and demanding
DOCTOR PROCTOR – handsome and charming
HARRY – anxious husband
SALLY – Harry's wife suffering from a mysterious aliment
PHYLLIS – demanding patient
BOB – hypochondriac looking for attention
BILL – hooked on prescription drugs

IN THE EMERGENCY WARD OF THE HOSPITAL.
NURSES TILLY AND TANSY ARE GOSSIPING.

TILLY: Did you hear? They found another dead body in the morgue this morning.

TANSY: Well that seems a reasonable place to find a dead body.

TILLY: Yes but the body belonged to someone who was alive yesterday right here in our emergency ward. It was Mrs Vanspangen.

TANSY: Mrs Vanspangen? Oh no! And I thought she was recovering so well after her operation on her bunions.

TILLY: She was. That's why it was surprising that she turned up in the morgue. And her bunions didn't explain how she managed to have that scalpel stuck in her back.

TANSY: Perhaps she had borrowed a scalpel to slice up some of the fruit that her friends had brought for her and then somehow accidentally fell over backwards and stabbed herself and staggered down into the morgue to save us the trouble of taking her there later.

TILLY: Maybe, but she also had a noose made from a hospital sheet tied around her neck.

TANSY: Well perhaps she was trying to mop up the blood from the scalpel wound and accidentally twisted the sheet around her neck.

TILLY: Maybe, but that doesn't explain how she had that syringe full of acid hanging out of her arm.

TANSY: Well perhaps…ENTER MATRON.

MATRON: What are you two standing there gossiping for? This is a hospital not a café and there are patients that need to be cared for.

TILLY: Not as many as there used to be. Mrs Vanspangen is gone. That makes four deaths in our ward in the past week.

MATRON: I don't want to hear any of your nonsense. It's a hospital. These things happen. Besides I won't miss her with all her carrying on about her bunions and how she wanted to get back to her ballroom dancing. I can't stand the way these patients mess up our lovely hospital beds sometimes. And on the subject of mess, get a move on and clean out the bed pans again. I want them polished so much I can see my face when I look in them.

TILLY: (To TANSY) They don't have to be clean for that.

MATRON: What was that?

TILLY: Oh nothing.

MATRON: Right. Now get to work….NOW!!! THEY LEAVE. ENTER THE YOUNG AND SWEET NEW NURSE NANCY. Who are you and what are you doing in my ward?

NANCY: Hello Matron. I am new Nurse Nancy. I was told to report to your ward.

MATRON: Well Nurse Nancy if you are going to be working here, you need to know a few of the rules. Rule one. Do as I say. Rule two. If you don't like what I say then remember rule one. Rule three. Never get involved with your patient. I try to make sure they are never here for long.

NANCY: Got it.

MATRON: Right now go and find a toothbrush and start cleaning the bits between the tiles in the staff toilet until you are needed for something else.

NANCY: Yes Matron. SUDDENLY THERE IS A LOT OF NOISE AND A WOMAN IS BROUGHT INTO THE WARD ACCOMPANIED BY HER WAILING HUSBAND.

HARRY: (Overacting badly) Oh woe oh disaster. Help, help, help!!! My wife has collapsed from some unknown ailment. Somebody help her. Oh oh oh!

MATRON: Don't just stand there like a stunned mullet Nurse. Go and prepare a bed for this patient. AS NURSE RUNS OUT SHE BUMPS INTO DOCTOR PROCTOR. THERE IS A

STUNNED MOMENT AS THEY LOOK INTO EACH OTHER'S EYES AND LOVE IS IN THE AIR.

NANCY: I'm sorry Doctor.

PROCTOR: No no it was my fault. You must be new here.

NANCY: Yes it's my first day. I'm Nurse Nancy

PROCTOR: I'm Doctor Proctor.

NANCY: Lovely to meet you Doctor Proctor.

MATRON: Doctor will you come here immediately!! This woman is in distress and her husband needs sedating!

HARRY: Yes oh please, please, please. Help my poor wife.

PROCTOR: What are her symptoms?

HARRY: Well she started coughing…then she ummm started to get a rash all over her then she started to get double vision. Suddenly she lost the use of her right arm and then she had really bad hiccups. Then she started to shake all over and then she dropped unconscious to the floor.

PROCTOR: Hmmmm. Mysterious. We better admit her straight away so I can run some tests.

HARRY: Thankyou Doctor. THEY ALL GO TO THE WARD WHERE ONE OTHER PATIENT IS SITTING UP READING A MAGAZINE.

PHYLLIS: What's all the fuss about? What is going on? Can't you see I'm trying to read?

HARRY: My wife is suffering from some mysterious disease. Her situation is desperate.

PHYLLIS: Oh that would be right. Some new patient comes in and suddenly all the attention goes to her. I've been waiting for five minutes for a cup of tea and do the Nurses care about that? Oh no, there's always someone else more important. ENTER NURSE NANCY. Nurse!! Where's my cup of tea?

NANCY: I'm sorry Mrs Farnsworth. I'll get it right away.

MATRON: Nurse! Get over here now and assist Doctor Proctor with his examination of Mrs Jones.

HARRY: Oh please help me. What is wrong with my wife? My poor, poor Sally.

PROCTOR: It might be better matron if Nurse Nancy looks after Mr Jones for the moment while we do the examination.

NANCY: Certainly Doctor. Come this way Mr Jones. Just sit down here a moment.

HARRY: Thankyou Nurse.

NANCY: I'm sure your wife will be alright.

HARRY: I hope so. I'd be lost without her. Oh I can't stand this happening. Oh why did it have to happen to Shirley of all people?

NANCY: Isn't your wife's name Sally?

HARRY: Um yes but I call her Shirley sometimes. Oh why, why?

NANCY: I know the Matron told me not to get involved in patients lives but I feel so sorry for you Mr Jones. Is there anything I can do to help?

HARRY: Just look after her. My life would be nothing without my Sandy.

NANCY: Wait here a moment. I'll be right with you. SHE EXITS.

PHYLLIS: What about me? I could be having a heart attack and none of you would notice. The worst place to go when you are sick is to a hospital if you ask me.

HARRY: What are you in for?

PHYLLIS: Well it started with complications from an ingrown toenail. Now they can't figure out what is wrong with me. They are hopeless. They keep sending me home then I get an attack and end straight back up in here. But can they help me? Do they care? No none of them. NANCY RE-ENTERS WITH A CUP OF TEA. Well it's about time.

NANCY: Here you are Mr Jones. I hope this makes you feel better.

HARRY: Thank you Nurse.

PHYLLIS: Oh that would be right. I've been waiting hours and I still don't get one.

NANCY: I'll get you one right now.

MATRON: Nurse! Stop wasting time and come over here and help us with this examination. And where is the rest of my useless staff? Don't they know it's an emergency? SCREAMS OUT. Where is everyone?!! ENTER TILLY AND TANSY.

TANSY: What is it Matron?

MATRON: Have you finished with the bedpans yet?

TILLY: Almost.

MATRON: Then hurry up with that then get here and help us with Mrs Jones.

PHYLLIS: And maybe one of you could get me a cup of tea?

HARRY: Have you discovered what is wrong with my wife yet Doctor?

PROCTOR: No not yet but she seems to be stable. NANCY ENTERS WITH THE TEA.

PHYLLIS: It's about time. BUT PROCTOR INTERCEPTS NANCY.

PROCTOR: Oh is that for me. Thank you Nurse.

NANCY: Oh that's alright Doctor Proctor.

PROCTOR: Call me Hector.

NANCY: I don't think I should while we are on duty.

PROCTOR: Well while we are on duty I suppose I must be just 'Doctor' to you but I hope that sometime soon you will see that I am not always Doctor Hector Proctor. Away from this hospital I am just an ordinary man.

MATRON: Is this a hospital or a kindergarten. Everyone get back to work. This place is enough to make you sick. Everyone, clear the room and let the patients rest. Nurse Nancy! I think that old Mister Hicks is due for his sponge bath. And don't worry about him getting frisky. I have been chilling his sponge in the fridge for the past hour. SHE LEAVES LAUGHING EVILLY.

TILLY: TO NANCY Don't worry about Matron. Everyone knows she is really just a pit bull terrier with lipstick.

TANSY: Don't be silly Tilly. She is not nearly as pretty as that.

PROCTOR: Nurse Nancy. Would you come and assist me on my rounds?

NANCY: I'd better check with matron first.

PROCTOR: I'll see you later then. THEY EXIT LEAVING HARRY WITH HIS WIFE AND PHYLLIS.

PHYLLIS: What about my CUP OF TEA!!!!

HARRY: You can have mine if you like?

PHYLLIS: You've got to be joking. I might catch something. I don't know where you've been.

HARRY: Well I'll find a Nurse to see about getting you your tea. HE EXITS.

PHYLLIS: Typical. Everyone runs off and forgets me. It happens all the time in this place. And look at her over there in the bed. All she does is lie there and everyone runs around giving her all the attention.

ENTER BOB. HE SLINKS AROUND, GOES OVER TO WHERE SALLY IS LYING AND STARTS TO LOOK AROUND SUSPICIOUSLY.

PHYLLIS: Hey what are you doing? He jumps up.

BOB: Hey, Who! Nothing lady. I was just looking for something. I've got this headache see so I came here to get something for it.

PHYLLIS: Well you won't find anything here. Get out of it or I'll call Matron.

BOB: Oh no. Not Matron! Don't do that. HE RUNS OUT. NANCY ENTERS TO CHECK ON SALLY. ENTER BILL.

BILL: Excuse me Nurse. Do you think you could help me? I have a splinter in my finger.

NANCY: I can call Doctor if you like.

BILL: No you'll be fine. It's only a splinter. But you might need to use a big needle. Or a knife. I don't mind.

NANCY: A knife?

BILL: And you can twist it a little bit if you like. I don't mind.

NANCY: But won't that hurt?

BILL: I don't mind. Really. In fact I think my appendix is hurting. It might burst. You better remove it. Look I'll just lay here and you can cut it out. Don't worry about anaesthetic. I don't mind.

51

NANCY: I really think I should call a Doctor. I'm not trained to operate on people.

BILL: Well maybe you can just give me an injection. Use the biggest needle you have. I don't mind.

NANCY: What is going on?

BILL: Do you want you use the defibrillator on me? I could do with a good electrical jolt right now. You can make it a big one. I don't mind.

NANCY: I think I better go and get Matron.

BILL: Matron? Look there's only so much pain that even I can stand. HE RUNS OUT. HARRY ENTERS WITH FLOWERS AND CHOCOLATES.

HARRY: I've brought these for my beloved Sarah. Just so she knows I care even if she is unconscious.

NANCY: Perhaps you can just put them on the table next to her bed. THEY DO SO.

PHYLLIS: That would be right. No-one ever brings me chocolates.

NANCY: Come on now Mr Jones. We'll find Doctor Proctor and see if he has any more news about your wife. THEY EXIT. PHYLLIS WAITS THEN GETS OUT OF BED, OPENS THE CHOCOLATES, PICKS THEM OUT ONE AT A TIME AND BITES A FEW OF THEM THEN PUTS THEM BACK. THEN SHE GRABS SALLY'S FLOWERS AND PUTS THEM ON THE TABLE NEXT TO HER BED.

PHYLLIS: What does she want flowers for? She's unconscious anyway. Now looks like I will have to get that cup of tea for myself. SHE EXITS. ENTER BOB.

BOB: Oh man, you'd think a place like this would have something for me. ENTER BILL. Hey man. How are you doing?

BILL: Hey Bob. It's not going well man. I can't get anyone to help me. All they want to do is give me something for the pain.

BOB: Well why don't you grab it man and give it to me.

BILL: Are you in pain?

BOB: No but I might be if I don't get something for it soon? ENTER NANCY.

NANCY: Can I help you?

BOB: Yes I'm in pain. Can you give me a pethidine injection?

NANCY: I'm afraid you'll have to see the Doctor for that.

BOB: Well can you tell me where you keep the pethidine. I don't want to bother the Doctor. I can do it myself.

NANCY: You'd have to ask Matron about that. BOB AND BILL LOOK AT EACH OTHER THEN RUN OUT. NANCY TURNS TO WHERE SALLY IS LYING. Oh you poor thing. Lying there all helpless. And your poor husband is so distraught. I know I shouldn't get involved with the patients but I feel so sorry about it all. What if something like this happened to me? Who would be there to bring me flowers and hold my hand until I got better again? ENTER PROCTOR.

PROCTOR: Ah Nurse Nancy. I was looking for you.

NANCY: What is it Doctor Proctor?

PROCTOR: I just wanted to make sure you were alright. I'm not sure if you know but there have been some strange goings on in this hospital. A number of patients have died in mysterious ways in the past few weeks and all of them here from this ward. I just want you to be extra careful.

NANCY: Oh don't worry about me Doctor Proctor.

PROCTOR: I can't help but worry about you Nancy. You're in my thoughts every minute.

NANCY: Oh Doctor Proctor you mustn't say these things.

PROCTOR: Call me Hector.

NANCY: Hector. You must know I feel the same way that you do – but this is not the time or place.

PROCTOR: You can't put me off forever. ENTER TILLY:

TILLY: Doctor. Come quickly. Someone has broken into the drugs store room and there is a man standing in the waiting room with his head stuck in the automatic door but every time we pull him out he sticks his head in it again.

PROCTOR: Good heavens. We better attend to this. THEY ALL EXIT. ENTER PHYLLIS.

PHYLLIS: Typical. No tea bags in the tea room. TURNS TO SALLY. And look at you lying there, waiting for the next lot of visitors and Doctors and Nurses to dance attendance on you.

You're as bad as that horrible woman Mrs Vanspangen who was in that bed before you. And all those others. It seems the only way I can ever get the attention I deserve here is to get rid of every other patient in this hospital. At least this won't be as hard as some of the others. You won't be able to put up much of a fight lying there. PHYLLIS GRABS A PILLOW AND GOES OVER TO SUFFOCATE SALLY. SALLY STARTS TO STRUGGLE AND SUDDENLY HARRY BURSTS INTO THE ROOM.

HARRY: Hold it right there. What do you think you're doing?

PHYLLIS: Nothing. I was going to prop up your wife's head with another pillow but I slipped and fell over. It was an accident but no harm done.

SALLY: That's what you think!!

PHYLLIS: Crikey! You got better quickly. NANCY ENTERS

NANCY: Oh look. You're conscious!! This is great news. I must get the others. SHE RUSHES OUT THEN ENTERS WITH MATRON, TWO NURSES AND PROCTOR.

PROCTOR: I must say this is a remarkable recovery!

SALLY: Not really. I was never sick in the first place!

ALL: What??!!!

SALLY: This is a police investigation relating to the suspicious deaths in the hospital over the past weeks. And it looks like we have found the culprit.

NANCY: What do you mean?

SALLY: Over there. That woman tried to suffocate me with a pillow when she thought no-one was around.

PHYLLIS: Yes it's true. And why not!! I was sick and tired of everyone else in this hospital getting more attention than me, it seemed that every time a new patient arrived everyone was there to make a fuss over them but I was just ignored. So there was only one way I could get the attention I deserved – get rid of every other patient in the hospital!

PROCTOR: You would never get away with it.

PHYLLIS: Oh wouldn't I?

HARRY: No you won't. You're under arrest!

PHYLLIS: Don't try any other of your tricky moves. SHE PULLS OUT A GUN I've got a gun and I'm not afraid to use it.

NANCY: What are we going to do now?

PHYLLIS: You are going to watch me walk out of here and there's no way you can stop me. AT THAT MOMENT BOB AND BILL ENTER FROM BEHIND. BOB IS HIGH AS A KITE AND STAGGERS INTO PHYLLIS.

BOB: I'm sorry sir. It is those damned pixies. They are crawling up the walls. AT THAT MOMENT HARRY AND SALLY JUMP FORWARD AND DISARM PHYLLIS.

PHYLLIS: Curses!

BILL: Hey what did she do? Can you do that to me too? Maybe push my arm right up my back. Please. Go on. I won't mind.

MATRON: That's enough of this nonsense. Everyone get back to work. I am trying to run a hospital here not a zoo.

HARRY: It's jail for you now.

PHYLLIS: Will I at least be able to get a hot cup of tea there? PHYLLIS, HARRY AND SALLY EXIT.

MATRON: TO THE NURSES. Well what are you two gawking at? It's time to empty the bedpans again I'm sure. And I have Mr Hollingsworth's enema to attend to. MATRON TILLY AND TANSY EXIT.

PROCTOR: Well Nurse Nancy. It's just you and me.

NANCY: What should we do now?

PROCTOR: Well I have an examination I would like you to assist me with.

NANCY: Oh. Who? Where?

PROCTOR: You. In the linen cupboard. Come on Nancy. HE GRABS HER HAND AND THEY RUN OUT.

THE END

ONE NIGHT…

CHARACTERS
(All 16 year old girls)
KELLY
SHELLY
KATE
KIM
CHLOE
SOPHIE
SALLY
SUZIE
SARAH
TANIA
THERESA

THE ACTION TAKES PLACE IN VAROUS ROOMS IN A SUBURBAN (KATE'S) HOME

SCENE ONE

KELLY: Can you take me home please?

SHELLY: Are you sure that's the best thing to do?

KELLY: Just take me home.

SHELLY: Come on now. I don't think just turning your back on everything and pretending it didn't happen is going to help.

KELLY: Easy for you to say.

SHELLY: You know what I mean.

KELLY: Do I? You think that me going back in there and facing them is going to make any difference? That they aren't all talking about it right now? Shaking their heads or laughing? I can hear them now. Poor Kelly. Poor stupid Kelly. I just can't do it.

SHELLY: Do you want a hug?

KELLY: I told you what I want. I want you to take me home. Take me away from it all.

SHELLY: And then what?

KELLY: I don't know.

SHELLY: You going to hide away in your room. Cut yourself off from the world like some tragic loser

KELLY: Why not? It's what the world thinks I am now isn't it? A tragic loser?

SHELLY: I just…umm I mean I don't think…

KELLY: Oh I'm sorry. Is it embarrassing you to be with me now? You want to distance yourself from what happened. Think you have better friends inside there?

SHELLY: Now you're being stupid.

KELLY: No. I was being stupid when I came here. The one good thing that has happened is that now I can see what a horrible world it is and I don't want to be part of it any more.

SHELLY: Surely if you went back in and explained...

KELLY: Me explain?!! What have I got to explain? It's her fault. Oh God when I think of the look on her face... that smug look.

SHELLY: I think she was as shocked as you were.

KELLY: No. She knew. It was planned like a military operation. She knew where the enemy was and where she could find allies. But.. oh Shelly I just want to disappear and never be seen again.

SHELLY: Don't you think you should at least talk to Matt?

KELLY: SCREAMING I don't even want to hear his name!!

SHELLY: But he's going to want to talk to you.

KELLY: He can rot in hell.

SHELLY: Come on. Thinking like that is not going to help the situation.

KELLY: Can't you see? Nothing is going to help the situation. Nothing can fix this. All those plans, all those dreams, they mean nothing now.

SHELLY: Maybe I can call someone to come and pick you up.

KELLY: Maybe you should.

SHELLY: It's not that I don't want to walk you home...

KELLY: Don't worry about it. I'll try and give my Mother a call.

SHELLY: And what are you going to tell her? She's going to be upset too.

KELLY: She'll just have to deal with it. It's not as if it's her life that's been ruined.

SHELLY: But still…

KELLY: What? What has it got to do with her in the end apart from giving her the chance to say I told you so? She said it was wrong. She said I needed to think about things more before I committed myself. Oh God I can't stand it. I can't even call Mum and go and hide at home when I think about it.

SHELLY: Your Mum's not like that.

KELLY: How would you know? You weren't there for the arguments in the first place. She'd say 'if you want my opinion..' and I'd tell her 'No I don't'. But she'd give it anyway. And the horrible, horrible thing is she was right all along.

SHELLY: So what are you going to do?

KELLY: I don't know. I don't know. All I know is I can't stay here any longer. I have to go.

SHELLY: I can't let you leave by yourself like this.

KELLY: Why not?

SHELLY: Because I'm your friend.

KELLY: Yeah but that's not likely to be a good thing to be after tonight. Go be her friend instead. Go be Matt's friend. I just want to be alone. KELLY EXITS.

SCENE TWO

KATE: What have you got there?

KIM: Nothing.

KATE: Don't lie to me. Show me what you were trying to hide under that cushion.

KIM: It's nothing I tell you. Go away.

KATE: And you expect me to believe you.

KIM: I expect you to trust me.

KATE: How am I supposed to trust you when you've been keeping secrets from me?

KIM: What's that supposed to mean?

KATE: Exactly what I said. I know you've been keeping secrets. You've been acting weird for a couple of weeks now.

KIM: I haven't been feeling well.

KATE: More lies.

KIM: I wouldn't have to make up stories if you weren't so suspicious and snooping around me all the goddamn time.

KATE: Well if you were honest and upfront with me like you used to be...

KIM: Things have changed.

KATE: How?

KIM: Everything's changed since two weeks ago.

KATE: Things only change if you let them change.

KIM: Easy for you to say. You don't have to deal with what I have to deal with every day.

KATE: Maybe. Maybe not. But that's no reason to stop trusting each other.

KIM: Why are you so interested suddenly in everything I do and say? You didn't used to be until two weeks ago. Since then you've been watching me like a hawk. You're starting to suffocate me. I can't move. I can't turn around except to find you there, staring at me, snooping around, asking questions.

KATE: Just tell me what you hid under the cushion just now.

KIM: And if I don't?

KATE: Suit yourself. It'll come out eventually. People talk Kim.

KIM: You don't have to remind me of that.

KATE: You didn't steal it did you?

KIM: Are you accusing me of stealing the...

KATE: I'm only asking. It wasn't you was it?

KIM: I can't believe you'd even ask me that. No, it wasn't me.

KATE: It's just you disappeared from the room just now so quickly.

KIM: I had to get out of there. It was suffocating. I wasn't the only one to leave.

KATE: Alright.

KIM: And as if I'd shove it behind a cushion. I'd be cleverer than that if I was going to steal it.

KATE: Which gets back to the question what have you hidden behind the cushion and why are you so determined to hide it from me. SHE MOVES TO HAVE A LOOK

KIM: You touch that cushion and I'll never speak to you again

KATE: Tell what it is.

KIM: NO!

KATE: TELL ME!

KIM: NO NO NO NO NO!!!

KATE: Fine. Suit yourself. Whatever it is, I hope you think it's worth it. SHE EXITS.

KIM: Kate, wait!! There's an explanation. Just trust me for a bit. Kate please….. ENTER CHLOE.

CHLOE: What's going on?

KIM: Nothing.

CHLOE: I heard you right through the door. What's wrong with Kate? She looked really upset.

KIM: I think everyone seems a bit upset don't you.

CHLOE: Maybe.

KIM: I better go and talk to her. SHE SNEAKS OVER AND GRABS SOMETHING FROM BEHIND THE CUSHION.

CHLOE: What's that?

KIM: What?

CHLOE: What did you just pick up from behind the cushion?

KIM: Nothing. I have to go and talk to Kate.

CHLOE: Show me.

KIM: Which way did she go?

CHLOE: Down that way. KIM EXITS. What is she hiding?

SCENE THREE.

SOPHIE: Six days to go.

SALLY: If we ever get there.

SUZIE: You can't let yourself think like that.

SARAH: Why not? We're all thinking it. Don't blame Sally just because she's the first one to say it out loud.

SUZIE: This is not the time to be negative.

SALLY: Why not? People are dropping like flies. You can't even start to guess who the next one to go will be. It could be any one of us.

SOPHIE: I'm scared.

SARAH: We're all scared. I guess the thing to do is watch each other's back. It's only six more days. Surely we can last that long.

SALLY: That's what the others were thinking I bet before tonight.

SUZIE: Well then how about we try and learn from what happened to them? The cracks have been there for months now. People are bound to fall through them. Just be glad it wasn't you.

SOPHIE: I had no idea it would be like this. I thought it would be fun. But so many have gone now.

SARAH: You should have realized this wasn't a game Sophie. This operation has been years in the planning. It's a military exercise, not a tea party. And in this kind of thing there are always casualties.

SALLY: I think maybe we should just disperse now. It seems to be that every time we all have got together that more of us get struck down. With six days to go maybe we should just keep our heads down and wait it out.

SOPHIE: I can't do it alone. I don't want to do it alone.

SALLY: None of us want to do it alone but maybe it's the best way to make sure we all make it through.

SUZIE: Perhaps we should just wait here. They might come back.

SARAH: Are you kidding?

SUZIE: Well maybe we shouldn't just assume the worst this time. Maybe there is some hope still.

SOPHIE: Do you really think they might come back Suzie?

SALLY: Or are you trying to keep us all here for some other reason.

SUZIE: What do you mean?

SALLY: Maybe there's some other nasty surprises in store for us and you want to make sure we're all here to enjoy them.

SUZIE: You're just being paranoid now.

SARAH: If some of the others had been more 'paranoid' as you call it they'd still be with us now.

SUZIE: Are you trying to say that I was somehow involved in all this?

SALLY: Well when you think about it, it all has to come from someone within the group. It has to be someone who knows us. Who is trusted by us. Who could get to know all our secrets and then go around picking us off one by one.

SOPHIE: You can't really think that Suzie is...

SARAH: Well it has to be one of us doesn't it?

SUZIE: No it doesn't. There are dozens of other people it could be. It might even be someone who doesn't even know us, just hates us and wants to make sure we disappear.

SALLY: Maybe. Maybe not. I'm not willing to take the risk. There's too much at stake. It's time to break this little party up once and for all.

SCENE FOUR.

TANIA: Are you happy with yourself?

THERESA: What are you talking about?

TANIA: I know what you did.

THERESA: Oh and what is it that I am supposed to have done.

TANIA: You left her for dead.

THERESA: You're not blaming me for what happened are you?

TANIA: Why shouldn't I when you are the one responsible.

THERESA: Well she had it coming.

TANIA: How can you say that?

THERESA: Because it's true.

TANIA: I'm going to tell everyone.

THERESA: They probably know already. And you know what? I don't care.

TANIA: But when everyone finds out...

THERESA: What? They gonna throw me in jail? They gonna drag me out in the streets and stone me to death? I don't care what they do.

TANIA: How can you be so heartless about it?

THERESA: It was going to be her or me, can't you see that? If I hadn't made the move then it would be her dancing on my grave.

TANIA: Couldn't you have reached a compromise?

THERESA: There's no compromise. It's the law of the jungle out there now. Kill or be killed.

TANIA: I can't believe it's come to this.

THERESA: Well don't blame me. Blame the world. Blame society. We're all just puppets in the game someone else set up. And whoever it is that's pulling the strings I'm just glad they pulled mine before she had a chance to get me first.

TANIA: So what now?

THERESA: I'll tell you what now. I'm going back in to face them all and see what happens. I might not be proud of what I did but I'm prepared to face the consequences.

TANIA: I wish there was another way.

THERESA: The path has been set. There's no turning back. Let's just play this little drama out until the final curtain goes down.

SHE MOVES INTO THE CENTRE AND **SCENE FIVE** SPRINGS TO

SALLY: Hi Theresa. I thought you'd gone home with all the others.

THERESA: No, I was just talking to Tania in the kitchen.

SUZIE: We were all just about to leave actually.

THERESA: How come?

SARAH: Well after the scene with Kelly. And it's not the first time something like this has happened.

TANIA: Was she still saying her life was over when she left?

SOPHIE: Yes it was awful. She was crying and saying her life was over and she wasn't even going to come next week.

TANIA: TO THERESA. Happy now?

THERESA: Nothing's changed. ENTER KATE.

KATE: What's everyone standing up looking like they're about to go? This is meant to be a party isn't it?

SALLY: Well it was but you know how these parties have been lately.

SOPHIE: I'm sorry Kate. I'm staying.

THERESA: Well I'm not going.

KATE: We really need to put on some music or something.

TANIA: Good idea. KIM AND CHLOE ENTER.

CHLOE: Hey Kate, how long ago was the pizza ordered? I'm starving.

KIM: You ordered pizza? On top of everything else? Am I the only person who is on a diet here?

KATE: Kim you so need to chill about your diet. You're becoming obsessed.

KIM: It's only for another six days. I'll never fit into my dress if I don't stick to the diet.

SALLY: Then you better stop sneaking the chocolate.

KIM: What?

SALLY: Nothing. It was a joke. ENTER SHELLY.

KATE: How is she Shelly?

SHELLY: Look she's gone home. Still going on about it being the end of her life and all that but I think she'll calm down.

SOPHIE: I just can't believe she reacted so badly to it.

TANIA: I know. But I think you'd better tell them Theresa.

SARAH: Tell us what?

THERESA: Alright then. There's no need to explain how important our dresses are for the Formal next Friday right?

ALL: Yeah. Of course. Right etc

THERESA: Well you know how Kelly had been going on and on about her designer dress and how it's a one off and everything. Well I just happened to see a picture of her dress a few weeks back and later when I was shopping I saw the same one in another store. It's a beautiful dress, perfect for me so...

SUZIE: You didn't!!

THERESA: Yes, I bought it for myself.

TANIA: Why would you do that?

THERESA: Well first of all I really liked it and out of all the dresses I had tried on it was by far the best one for me.

SALLY: But the same dress!

THERESA: Well she shouldn't have been carrying on for so long about hers being so perfect and a one off and everything. Well maybe there was only one of them in size 12 but mine is a size 10.

CHLOE: That's kind of cruel Theresa.

THERESA: Well I gave her fair warning. When we were all showing pictures of our dresses before she had the chance to see what I was wearing…

SHELLY: Well you know what. It's about time this all stopped. We're meant to be friends and the Formal is meant to be one of the best nights of our life and for months we've been treating it like it was preparing for a terrorist attack. Maybe you shouldn't have copied her dress Theresa but she shouldn't have acted as if you had just blown up her house either. All we've been doing for months is making ourselves stressed and miserable about the stupid Formal.

KATE: Exactly. This party was meant to be a time for us to enjoy getting ready for it, not turn into some stupid drama.

KIM: You're right you know. And you know what else. I'm starving. And while I'm waiting for the pizza to get here I'm going to eat this. SHE PULLS OUT A CHOCOLATE BAR.

SUZIE: So that's where the Kit Kat that was in the fridge got to.

KIM: Yep and I don't care. Kate, get some music on. This is meant to be a party. KELLY APPEARS AT THE DOOR.

KELLY: Hi guys.

THERESA: Hi Kelly. I'm glad you've come back.

KELLY: Thanks.

THERESA: I'm sorry about the dress.

KELLY: Really it's ok. I thought it actually made my backside look big anyway. And Mum just told me of this great little shop that has had these new designer dresses just come in. So it's ok. I mean, it's important we wear something that suits us right.

ALL: Right. THE MUSIC COMES UP AND THE PARTY STARTS. THERESA DRAGS TANIA TO ONE SIDE.

THERESA: That dress doesn't make my backside look big does it?

THE END

SNOW WHITE AND THE SEVEN SINS

CHARACTERS
MAGIC MIRROR
QUEEN
SNOW WHITE
WOODCUTTER
SLOTHY
LUSTY
VANITY
ENVY
ANGRY
GLUTTONY
GREEDY
PRINCE

MIRROR: Once upon a time….look before I even begin I have to ask, what is it with this 'once upon a time' rubbish? What does it actually mean? That's the whole problem with this fairy tale scene. No-one actually stops to ask why. Why are there talking animals and handsome princes and wicked stepmothers and dark forests? And why are there talking magic mirrors? Still I suppose I shouldn't question that too much in case I find out I don't really exist, which just all gets too existential for everyone concerned. So anyway, as you can see I'm a talking magic mirror, so I guess you know what is going to happen next. ENTER QUEEN.

QUEEN: Mirror mirror on the wall. Who's the fairest of them all?

MIRROR: Why do you want to ask a question like that? Don't you already know you're a hottie your majesty.

QUEEN: But I need to be sure that I am the fairest in the land. Without my looks I'm just a vain, psychotic woman who dabbles in witchcraft so it's important that I am the most beautiful thing going so that people don't notice some of my less appealing personality disorders.

MIRROR: But what's wrong with being just one of the most beautiful.

QUEEN: You're avoiding the question. Just give me the answer or I'll risk the seven years bad luck and throw a brick at you.

MIRROR: Alright, alright. Don't get your tiara in a twist. Here you go then. Though you are very fair, tis true, Snow White is far more fair than you.

QUEEN: WHAT!!!

MIRROR: You asked for it.

QUEEN: I knew it. That little tramp, skipping around the castle all day, playing all innocent when all the time she was planning to take my place.

MIRROR: Are you sure? She is your husband the King's daughter from his first marriage. I don't think she has any designs on your job.

QUEEN: Enough from you. I need to take care of this right now. SCREAMS OUT. Snow White! Get here NOW! SNOW WHITE SKIPS IN.

SNOW: Did I hear you calling me step mother dearest as I skipped in an innocent and girlish fashion around the castle.

QUEEN: Yes you did. I want you to do something for me. You know the dark, dark forest?

SNOW: You mean the one that surrounds the castle?

QUEEN: Yes that's the one. I was wondering if you could go into the middle of it and tell me what it's like.

SNOW: But I'm not supposed to go into the deep dark forest. It's full of scary things and I might get lost.

QUEEN: Listen Snow, you might be a pretty young princess but I'm the boss here so you'll do as you're told. I want you to go and find the middle of the deep dark forest and I want you to go NOW! Do you understand me?

SNOW: Alrighty. But Daddy will be very cross if I get lost and am never seen again.

QUEEN: You just leave your Father to me dear. Now off you trot.

SNOW: Very well. SNOW WHITE EXITS. QUEEN TURNS TO THE MIRROR.

QUEEN: Now that wasn't that hard was it. Let's see how things stand now. Mirror, mirror on the wall, who's the fairest of them all?

MIRROR: Though you are very fair, tis true, Snow White is far more fair than you.

QUEEN: What??!!

MIRROR: Well what did you expect Queenie? You just sent Snow White for a stroll in the woods. She's not going to be suddenly less pretty than you by getting some fresh air and exercise is she?

QUEEN: Well this calls for more drastic action. CALLS Woodcutter! Get here NOW!

ENTER WOODCUTTER.

WOODCUTTER: Umm, did somebody call me?

QUEEN: Yes you dolt. I have a job for you.

WOODCUTTER: Well thank you very much your majesty but I already have a job. I'm a woodcutter.

QUEEN: I imagine you practice on your own head.

WOODCUTTER: No because when I hit my head with my axe it hurts.

QUEEN: Whatever. Listen I have a job for you as well as woodcutting. You know the princess Snow White?

WOODCUTTER: You mean the pretty girl who skips around the palace all day long smiling and singing?

QUEEN: Yes that's her.

WOODCUTTER: Who dances and laughs and looks after cute little puppies and lights up the room when she walks into it.

QUEEN: Yes, yes. You've got the one.

WOODCUTTER: The one who is the most beautiful creature that this castle has ever seen.

QUEEN: That's enough! Look, here's an easy job for you. She has gone into the woods. All you have to do is follow her and whack her on the head with your axe.

WOODCUTTER: But that won't be good for her.

QUEEN: Well the idea is that you have to kill her.

WOODCUTTER: Why would I want to do that?

QUEEN: Because I am the Queen and you are a woodcutter and you have to do as I say.

WOODCUTTER: Well I can't argue with that.

QUEEN: Right so off you go and don't come back until you are sure she is dead. HE EXITS. It's so hard to get good help nowadays. SHE EXITS.

MIRROR: Well the woodcutter catches up to Snow White in the forest, as she really hadn't gone very far. When he finds her however things don't exactly go according to the Queen's evil plan. ENTER SNOW WHITE SINGING AND DANCING. THE WOODCUTTER FOLLOWS HER. HE SNEAKS UP BEHIND HER WITH HIS AXE RAISED. SHE TURNS.

SNOW: Oh hello there Mr. Woodcutter. Are you having a lovely day?

WOODCUTTER: Not too bad. And you?

SNOW: I'm having a delightful day thank you. At first when I was told to go into the woods I was a little frightened but it's actually quite pretty and lots of room to sing and dance.

WOODCUTTER: Well I'd be having a better day if I hadn't been told to go and whack somebody on the head with my axe.

SNOW: Gosh that's not very nice. Who is the poor person who is going to have your axe imbedded in their skull?

WOODCUTTER: You I'm afraid.

SNOW: Oh no. Please don't do that Mr. Woodcutter. I'm sure it would hurt and I wouldn't be able to sing and dance around if I had an axe in my head.

WOODCUTTER: Yes and that would be a pity.

SNOW: Well what are we to do? Neither of us wants your axe in my head I feel so we must think of a way out of this unfortunate situation.

WOODCUTTER: Don't look at me for an idea Snow White. I haven't had an idea since the axe head flew off its handle and hit me between the eyes while I was chopping down a tree years ago.

SNOW: Oh you poor man. Are you going to get in trouble if you don't kill me?

WOODCUTTER: I reckon I'll get in big trouble.

SNOW: Well it looks like there is no way out. I guess I'll just have to let you….wait a minute POINTING. What is that cottage I see in the clearing through there?

WOODCUTTER: I have never seen it before.

SNOW: Well how about this for a plan. You go back and pretend you have chopped my head off and I go and stay in that cottage forever and never come back.

WOODCUTTER: That sounds like it could work.

SNOW: Alright then. That's what we'll do. Goodbye friendly woodcutter and thank you for not burying your axe in my skull.

WOODCUTTER: Goodbye Snow White and good luck. HE EXITS.

SNOW: Well now let's see who lives in this cottage. SHE EXITS.

MIRROR: Now being a princess in a castle for her entire life, Snow White hadn't learned that inviting yourself into a strange house in the middle of a forest isn't necessarily the smartest thing to do. As it turned out this cottage belonged to a family of seven brothers and when you're a pretty girl and you are in the house of seven brothers who haven't seen a woman in years you could find yourself in a difficult situation, especially as the surname of these brothers was Sin. Oblivious to it all, Snow White let herself into the house and, tired out from all the exercise of walking through the forest, she falls asleep on the couch. SNOW WHITE IS ASLEEP AS THE SEVEN SINS COME HOME.

SINS: "Hi Ho, hi ho. Its home from sin we go,
 We lie, we cheat,
 We drink, we eat,
 Hi ho hi ho, hi ho hi ho".

SLOTHY: Hey what's going on? There is someone lying on my couch. Where am I supposed to lie down? I'm exhausted.

LUSTY: When aren't you exhausted Slothy? But because I'm such a kind brother I might help you this once and take this person up to my room to get her out of your way.

VANITY: That would be right Lusty. Any excuse to get her alone with you. Well if you have any hope you better get her out of this room before she wakes up and sees me. I'm so hot that if she sees me I'll be the only one she'll be interested in.

ENVY: I'm sick of you always talking about yourself Vanity. I hate it that I'm not as good looking as you. Or as pretty as her. Or as tall as him. In fact I hate you all.

ANGRY: Shut up Envy. You make me sick with your stupid carry on all the time. I am going to punch your lights out.

GREEDY: Calm down Angry. I think we need to look carefully at who we have here. Pretty girl. Nice clothes. Obviously from a family with money. Perhaps she got lost and her family will give a reward for us finding her. Or maybe hold her to ransom and get even more money.

GLUTTONY: I don't care about the money Greedy. As long as she is gone before dinner. I'm not going to share any of my food. There's not enough as it is.

ANGRY: Shut up Gluttony. There's plenty of food.

GLUTTONY: There's never enough food. And don't tell me to shut up.

SLOTHY: Yeah you always tell people to shut up.

ANGRY: Shut up Slothy. I do not always tell people to shut up.

LUSTY: You do so… THEY ALL DISOLVE INTO A BIG ARGUMENT THAT WAKES SNOW WHITE UP.

SNOW: What's going on? Who are you people?

LUSTY: I am your dream come true. A big bucket of love waiting for you to dip your feet into.

ENVY: That would be right. Ignore me and give the pretty girl all the attention.

SLOTHY: We are the seven Sins and you have forced your way into our house and onto my couch. Now get lost so I can lie down. I've never been so tired.

SNOW: The seven Sins? Goodness me, how alarming.

VANITY: Don't be frightened. You have nothing to fear from us and I certainly have nothing to fear from you. You might be pretty but I am the one who everyone wants to look at.

SNOW: You sound just like my step mother.

VANITY: Well what a charming and well spoken person she must be.

SNOW: Not really.

ANGRY: Shut up. Look whoever you are. How dare you break into our house and start asking questions like it's us who have done something wrong. This is ridiculous! It makes me so mad when people do things like that.

GLUTTONY: Don't worry. It makes him mad when people do anything at all. Listen. I don't care why you are here. Have you got anything to eat on you? I'm starving.

SNOW: No, nothing I'm afraid. I didn't have time to pack any food when my step mother sent me off into the forest to be killed by the wood cutter.

LUSTY: Well I think we should keep her here to protect and care for her.

GREEDY: The first thing we'll have to protect her from is you Lusty. But I reckon we should keep her here for a bit just in case we can get something for her later. Plus if she does the house work it will save money on hiring a house keeper. ALL THE SINS AGREE.

SLOTHY: Right now that's settled I'm off to have a nap. THE SINS HEAD OFF SINGING

SINS: "Hi Ho, hi ho. It's off to sin we go,
We lie, we cheat,
We drink, we eat,
Hi ho hi ho, hi ho hi ho".

SNOW: Well I guess I better get about cleaning this messy house. SHE EXITS.

MIRROR: And so it was that the seven Sins got an unpaid housekeeper to try and sort out their lives, which wasn't easy for Snow White as you can imagine. Still, while she was there she was safe from the wicked Queen. Or so she thought. ENTER THE QUEEN.

QUEEN: Well hasn't life been lovely since that wretched girl stopped hanging around the castle annoying everyone with her endless smiling and dancing about. And of course it gives everyone the opportunity to focus on me and how beautiful I am. I can never get enough hearing about how I'm the most gorgeous thing about. In fact, it's been a while since I gave my old friend the magic mirror a shot. GOES UP TO THE MIRROR. Mirror, mirror on the wall. Who's the fairest of them all?

MIRROR: Is this a trick question?

QUEEN: No. I would have thought the answer is obvious.

MIRROR: Can I phone a friend?

QUEEN: Stop beating around the bush. You know the answer. So tell me straight out and we can both get on with the day.

MIRROR: Are you sure?

QUEEN: Where did I put that brick?

MIRROR: Alright, Alright. Boy, someone got out of the wrong side of bed this morning. Umm what was the question again?

QUEEN: Who is the fairest of them all you fool?

MIRROR: Right. Oh well. Here goes. Though you are very fair, tis true, Snow White is far more fair than you.

QUEEN: What??!!

MIRROR: Just giving you the facts lady.

QUEEN: But she is dead! I sent the woodcutter myself to dispose of her. Oh that idiot must have gone all mushy and lied to me. Strange, I wouldn't have thought he had the brains for that.

MIRROR: Life's full of little surprises.

QUEEN: Where is that woodcutter? SCREAMS. Woodcutter!! Get here NOW! ENTER THE WOODCUTTER. Now I want you to tell me what's going on?

WOODCUTTER: What's going on with what your majesty?

QUEEN: I sent you into the woods to whack Snow White on the head with an axe did I not?

WOODCUTTER: Yes, I can safely say that is exactly what you sent me into the woods to do.

QUEEN: And I suppose you are going to tell me now that you did remove her head from the rest of her.

WOODCUTTER: I can safely say I took care of things and you'll never see her again.

QUEEN: You surprise me with your cunning woodcutter but I am a mistress of magic and I have discovered that you have deceived me and that Snow White is still alive.

WOODCUTTER: Oops yeah well I might not have exactly killed her.

QUEEN: Where is she?

WOODCUTTER: I'm not saying. She told me when she went to stay in the cottage in the woods that she would keep away and never come back. You'll never find her in the cottage in the woods because I'll never tell you that's where she is.

QUEEN: Ah ha! So she is in the cottage in the woods.

WOODCUTTER: How did you know that? Oh how will Snow White ever be safe from a witch as cunning and powerful as you.

QUEEN: Just get out you ninny and leave me alone to hatch a devious plot to get rid of Snow White once and for all. WOODCUTTER EXITS. Now what to do? Shoot her? No too messy. Strangle her? No, I'd leave fingerprints. Arrange for a plane to drop a bomb on her? Too obvious. Ah ha! I have it. I shall inject an apple with deadly poison and then dress as an old lady and trick her into eating it. What a cunning, straightforward and obvious way to get rid of someone you don't want around. Right, I'm off. SHE EXITS.

MIRROR: And so it was the wicked Queen hatched her evil plot to be rid of Snow White forever. Meanwhile Snow White was finding her hands full living with the seven Sins.

SNOW WHITE ENTERS SCREAMING BEING CHASED BY LUSTY.

LUSTY: Come on Snow White. Just one kiss. ANGRY ENTERS AND PUNCHES LUSTY IN THE FACE.

ANGRY: That's for making so much noise! ENTER THE OTHERS.

SLOTHY: Snow White you haven't tied my shoe laces for me yet.

VANITY: What do you do with your time Snow White. Why haven't you polished my mirror?

GREEDY: I still reckon we'd get a good price for her if we tried to sell her.

ENVY: Why does she get all the attention? Ever since Snow White got here no one pays any attention to me at all. Typical.

GLUTTONY: Where is my second breakfast? I've already finished my first and everyone's leftovers. You know how I like a second breakfast before heading off in the morning. THEY ALL START COMPLAINING LOUDLY.

SNOW WHITE: YELLS Quiet! THEY ALL FALL SILENT. Right boys I have one thing to say to you. It's time for work. MUTTERINGS OF WHAT? OH YES! TIME TO GET GOING. Right then everyone. Have a nice day. THEY EXIT

SINS: SINS: "Hi Ho, hi ho. It's off to sin we go,
We lie, we cheat,
We drink, we eat,
Hi ho hi ho, hi ho hi ho".

SNOW WHITE: Lovely boys but they can be a bit demanding at times. Oh well, better get on with the day's chores. ENTER THE WITCH DRESSED AS AN OLD WOMAN.

WITCH: Excuse me young lady. Could I beg a moment of your time?

SNOW: Certainly. How can I help you?

WITCH: ASIDE Oh it's too easy. She is so simple and trusting. TO SNOW WHITE. I am from the Forest Apple Growers

Association. I am doing a special apple survey in the neighbourhood. I have a lovely apple here which I am getting people to try and then rate on a scale of 1 to 10 according to how delicious and juicy they think it is.

SNOW: So you want me to taste that lovely shiny apple and then tell you how much I like it.

WITCH: Exactly.

SNOW: Certainly. SHE TAKES A BITE OF THE APPLE. Hmmm Sweet, crunchy with an unusual flavour on the back palate. I would give this apple a score of… SHE DROPS TO THE GROUND.

WITCH: Well that was easy enough. Now to get out of these rags and go back to the castle to gloat. SHE EXITS.

MIRROR: Well of course this is the part of the story when everyone thinks it's all over and we can say goodbye to Snow White forever. But of course, being a fairy tale, that wasn't the case. Just watch to see what happens when the Sins come home. ENTER THE SINS.

SINS: "Hi Ho, hi ho. Its home from sin we go,
We lie, we cheat,
We drink, we eat,
Hi ho hi ho, hi ho hi ho".

SLOTHY: Look at Snow White lying on the ground there. She is nearly as slothful as I am sleeping on the job.

ENVY: That's right. Everyone gets a rest but me.

ANGRY: Shut up you jealous idiot. Can't you see she's not breathing?

VANITY: She doesn't make nearly as good looking a corpse as I would.

GREEDY: Well if she's carked it then maybe we can sell of her body parts to a hospital.

LUSTY: She looks so lovely there. Perhaps I can give her one last kiss goodbye.

GREEDY: Hang on. What's that in her hand? An apple. Great, I feel like a snack. HE GRABS THE APPLE AND TAKES A BITE. Ooh, what an unusual taste. It reminds me of… HE DROPS TO THE GROUND.

ANGRY: Oh great. Two bodies to bury. ENTER THE PRINCE.

PRINCE: Forsooth and well met strange fellows. I am a Prince seeking love and adventure and a stranger in these parts. Couldst thou tell me which way to the castle which I believe is in the vicinity?

ENVY: Look as his clothes. I bet they cost a fortune and here I am dressed in rags. Typical.

PRINCE: What is this sight that blights mine eyes? It is a maiden fairer than any I have ever seen. And yet she lies so still, as if in death's cold embrace.

VANITY: Is this guy for real?

PRINCE: Let me closer oh strange and varied gentlemen. I wouldn't fain gaze upon her still yet beautiful visage. Oh how my heart breaks to see such beauty stilled forever.
THE PRINCE MOVES FORWARD TO GET CLOSER TO SNOW WHITE BUT TRIPS OVER THE BODY OF GLUTTONY. Oh bugger! HE FALLS ON SNOW WHITE WHICH DISLODGES THE APPLE IN HER THROAT. THE KICK ALSO MAKES GLUTTONY THROW UP HIS APPLE. THE TWO OF THEM COME TO.

SNOW WHITE: What happened?

PRINCE: A miracle. A miracle has happened. I came seeking love and beauty and have found them here. I may be a rich and powerful prince but in your presence I am but a humble servant, begging for your hand in marriage.

SNOW: Well this is all a bit sudden. But as long as you don't have seven sets of smelly feet so I have seven sets of smelly socks to wash every night I'm yours. It's a better deal than I am getting here with this lot.

PRINCE: Then up on my trusty steed fair maiden and back to my castle. SHE LOOKS AROUND BUT THERE IS NO HORSE. HE PULLS OUT COCONUT HALVES AND WITH HER RIGHT BEHIND HIM THE SEVEN SINS WAVING GOODBYE THEY CLIP CLOP OFF INTO THE DISTANCE.

GLUTTONY: What did I miss?

LUSTY: That Prince just came along and stole our Snow White away. That's what just happened.

GLUTTONY: Oh well. More dinner for us then. And what's this apple laying here? Who would leave a lovely piece of fruit lying around half eaten? HE GOES TO EAT IT AGAIN BUT THE OTHERS STOP HIM.

MIRROR: And well that just leaves the Wicked Queen to deal with. Well of course once she gets back to the castle you can imagine she would be in a real hurry to get to see me and ask me that same question again. And of course, with Snow White rescued, I guess I'll just have to tell her she's still number two.

SINS: No!!

MIRROR: No?

ANGRY: None of this would ever have happened if you just kept your big mouth shut.

MIRROR: Well what do you expect me to do?

GREEDY: Lie of course. Take the easy way out.

MIRROR: What do you think I am? A politician?

VANITY: Sometimes for the sake of a happily ever after ending a little white lie is necessary.

MIRROR: Ok. I get you. Not a bad bit of advice. Let me try it. Here she comes. THE SINS DISPERSE. ENTER THE QUEEN.

QUEEN: This time for sure! Mirror mirror on the wall. Who's the fairest of them all?

MIRROR: umm errr. You are Queeny.

QUEEN: You mean it?

MIRROR: Yeah. Whatever.

QUEEN: Oh at last. No more envy or vanity for me. I used to get so angry thinking about how I wanted to own all of the beauty in the land that I would lay around slothfully all day feasting on my desires. Now those sins are purged just by this peace of mind, knowing I'm the fairest. I swear I will never ask that question again and I will change my ways. Thank you so much mirror. SHE SKIPS OUT CHEERFULLY.

MIRROR: And I guess you could say after that they all lived happily ever after.

THE END

HUSH

CHARACTERS
KELLY
MATT
DAD
MUM
LAURA
MEGAN
EMILY
GO FIGURE
CHERYL

KELLY AND MATT COME ON STAGE AT THE END OF WHAT HAS BEEN A BIG ARGUMENT

MATT: So what is it you DO want then?

KELLY: I want you to listen to me.

MATT: I AM listening to you.

KELLY: No you're not. You're hearing me but that isn't the same as listening to me. When I said I wanted you to take me home and not go out after the party with the others what did you think I was saying?

MATT: I thought you were saying you were bored and didn't like my mates and didn't want anyone to have any fun, which is close to the truth.

KELLY: Where did you pull that from?

MATT: From the fact you were giving me dirty looks even before the party was finishing up. From the fact you were refusing to talk to Robbo. From the fact you kept looking at your watch and making a big show of it.

KELLY: Matt, all I was saying is I didn't want to go out afterwards. If you stopped to listen to why for a second...

MATT: From the fact you never want to kick on even if you are having a great time. From the fact that you always are the first to leave a party. From the fact that you look down your nose at people who are just having fun.

KELLY: Matt this is so unfair. I just said I wanted to go home. I didn't say you couldn't kick on.

MATT: Yeah and how does that look – me always going out without my girlfriend.

KELLY: It looks like you have a girlfriend who isn't allowed to stay out as late as everyone else.

MATT: I've heard that one so many times.

KELLY: Then why don't you listen when I say it to you?

MATT: Forget it Kelly. Call me when you grow up a little and stand up for yourself.

MATT EXITS. KELLY GOES IN TO SEE HER PARENTS, FURIOUS.

DAD: And what time do you think this is?

KELLY: Time I went to bed. Goodnight.

DAD: Just a minute. What time are you supposed to be home on the weekend?

KELLY: Midnight.

DAD: And what time do you call this?

KELLY: I dunno. Quarter past twelve.

DAD: It's 12.23

KELLY: Big deal.

MUM: We've been getting worried about you Kelly.

KELLY: Mum it's only 20 minutes. I was already the first person to come home. Everyone else is still out having a good time.

DAD: I don't care what everyone else is doing.

KELLY: Dad, I'm the only girl in my entire year level who has a midnight curfew. Don't you think maybe it's time you trusted me a little bit.

MUM: It's not you we don't trust darling it's...KELLY JOINS IN everyone else.

KELLY: I know but why do you think I'm more likely to get molested by a bikie gang or slipped a drug and left in a gutter before midnight. It's not as if all the freaks don't come out before then.

DAD: I'm not talking about that. This is about you being late.

KELLY: Dad. How about you listen to me for a minute.

DAD: I'm not going to listen to you until you can do what you're told.

KELLY: PLEADING. Mum…

DAD: You're Father's right Kelly.

KELLY: STORMING OUT. Oh what's the point?

KELLY GOES INTO HER ROOM WHERE THREE OF HER FRIENDS ARE WAITING. THE MOVEMENT STARTS TO BECOME A BIT MORE STYLISED AS WE SLIP FROM THE REALITY INTO THE INSIDE OF KELLY'S HEAD.

LAURA: Hi Kelly

MEGAN: Hi Kelly

EMILY: Hi Kelly.

KELLY: What are you doing here?

LAURA: Hi Kelly

MEGAN: Hi Kelly

EMILY: Hi Kelly.

KELLY: Hey stop that. Just tell me how you got in here.

LAURA: Hi Kelly

MEGAN: Hi Kelly

EMILY: Hi Kelly.

KELLY: Stop it! The joke's over.

LAURA: Sorry. Did you say something Kelly?

KELLY: How did you manage to talk my parents into letting you in? It must be getting on to 1 am?

MEGAN: It was easy. They didn't hear us.

KELLY: Weren't you going out with the guys?

EMILY: Nah, we wanted to make sure you were ok.

KELLY: I'm fine.

LAURA: But how are you?

KELLY? I'm fine.

MEGAN: How are you feeling?

KELLY: I'm fine I said.

THE GIRLS: You poor thing.

KELLY: What are you talking about?

EMILY: Everyone knows how unhappy you are at home.

KELLY: I'm not unhappy. Sure I get mad at this curfew thing but I'm not unhappy.

LAURA: And we know that you're unhappy so we're here for you.

KELLY: What's with you?

MEGAN: It's about you being unhappy. Everyone is talking about it.

KELLY: Well everyone can mind their own damned business because I'm NOT unhappy.

GIRLS: You poor thing.

KELLY: TRIES TO SCREAM IT OUT AT THEM BUT IT COMES OUT HALF SILENT. ... Not .... Hap...!! SHE LOOKS BEWILDERED.

EMILY: It's your parents isn't it. Everyone says so.

KELLY: No it's got nothing to... THE REST OF THE LINE IS MOUTHED BUT NOT AUDIBLE... do with my parents.

LAURA: It's to do with Matt isn't it?

KELLY: NO SOUND AT FIRST Matt has **nothing to do with it.**

MEGAN: Did you say something Kelly?

THE SCENE DISSOLVES INTO A MOVEMENT PIECE WHICH BEGINS WITH KELLY TRYING TO MAKE HERSELF HEARD AND MOVES FROM THE STRANGE SCENE WITH HER FRIENDS TO REPEATING THE SCENE WITH HER PARENTS AND THE SCENE WITH MATT IN A VERY STYLISED MANNER. EVERYONE IS DEAF TO

KELLY'S ATTEMPTS TO COMMUNICATE WITH THEM UNTIL KELLY IS LEFT SILENTLY SCREAMING. AS SHE IS LEFT ALONE HER VOICE SUDDENLY KICKS IN AND HER SCREAM RINGS OUT. SHE STOPS AND STANDS STUNNED AND CONFUSED. A FIGURE ENTERS AND LOOKS KELLY UP AND DOWN.

GO FIGURE: No need to scream. I can hear you perfectly.

KELLY: I'm having a nightmare. That's what's going on right?

GO FIGURE: If you say so.

KELLY: Well what else could it be?

GO FIGURE: Well then it's obviously a nightmare. So relax.

KELLY: How am I supposed to relax? And who are you?

GO FIGURE: I'm no-one.

KELLY: I don't get it. I know all the people that I have been dreaming about so far apart from you.

GO FIGURE: Go figure.

KELLY: No explanations? GO FIGURE SHRUGS. Fine. Well I guess I just sit here and wait till I wake up.

GO FIGURE: Suit yourself. THEY SIT THERE AWKWARDLY FOR A WHILE IN SILENCE.

KELLY: So, where do you come from?

GO FIGURE: Nowhere. Everywhere.

KELLY: You know what I can't quite figure. The part when I actually fell asleep? I remember the party. I remember getting home and the fight with Mum and Dad. Then that weird trippy thing with my friends. I guess it was somewhere around there but it's still confusing where real life stopped and the nightmare began.

GO FIGURE: Well you wouldn't be the first person to feel like that.

KELLY: I was having a bad enough night before all this happened.

GO FIGURE: And what was making your night so bad?

KELLY: I was just having hassles with my boyfriend and then with my parents and then with my friends, or at least I think it was my friends....I'm not sure.

GO FIGURE: What kind of hassles?

KELLY: It was crazy. People just weren't listening. Like I was trying to talk to them but they just weren't listening to me.

GO FIGURE: How awful.

KELLY: Yes it was.

GO FIGURE: It's the kind of thing you would never want to have happen to anyone really isn't it.

KELLY: Totally.

GO FIGURE: Can I show you something that happened after school yesterday?

KELLY: What's that got to do with anything?

GO FIGURE: Maybe nothing. Maybe something. You won't know until we take a look.

KELLY IS TALKING TO HER FRIENDS ABOUT MUSIC WHEN A NEW GIRL, CHERYL COMES UP. SHE STANDS ON THE OUTSIDE OF THE GROUP LOOKING FOR AN OPPORTUNITY TO JOIN THE CONVERSATION, THEN FINALLY SENSES A MOMENT AND JUMPS IN.

CHERYL: I really love Taylor Swift. She is like, so cool. I love her music. KELLY LOOKS AT HER AND DISMISSS HER AND KEEPS TALKING TO HER FRIENDS. THE CONVERSATION TURNS TO MOVIES. CHERYL HANGS BACK LOOKING AGAIN FOR AN OPPORTUNITY TO JOIN IN.

CHERYL: Yeah Liam Hemsworth is such a spunk. I love every movie I've seen him in.

THE GROUP JUST IGNORES CHERYL AND WALKS AWAY. SHE IS LEFT STANDING ALONE AND AS SHE GOES OFF DEJECTED AND STARTING TO CRY. KELLY COMES BACK ON.

KELLY: Hey wait. You there.

CHERYL: Are you talking to me?

KELLY: You can hear me?

CHERYL: Why wouldn't I be able to hear you?

KELLY: It's just... oh never mind. My name's Kelly.

CHERYL: I know.

KELLY: What's your name?

CHERYL: Cheryl.

KELLY: Have we met?

CHERYL: Yeah, a few times. Well maybe not met but I have seen you around school heaps of times.

KELLY: Right.

CHERYL: There are always so many people around you though. You're so popular. You would never have noticed me.

KELLY: I'm sorry. You should have just come up and said hello.

CHERYL: I did. You didn't hear me.

KELLY: Well I can hear you now.

CHERYL: Yeah I guess you can.

KELLY: You want to come and join the others?

CHERYL: I'd like to but I really need to get home.

KELLY: Ok well I guess I'll see you around. Hey, would you like to come to a party tomorrow night?

CHERYL: Are you sure? I would love to.

KELLY: Of course I'm sure.

CHERYL: Thanks. That would be awesome. See you. SHE EXITS. GO FIGURE ENTERS.

GO FIGURE: That wasn't so hard was it?

KELLY: Not at all.

GO FIGURE: Well I guess my job is done then. I'll let you get back to sleep. The sun will be up soon. Have a good day. After all it is Saturday today and you have a party to go to tonight. GO FIGURE EXITS.

THE END

FIFTEEN MINUTES OF FAME

CHARACTERS
CYNTHIA FERGUSON
MOTHER FERGUSON
FATHER FERGUSON
COUSIN ONE
COUSIN TWO
FRIEND ONE
FRIEND TWO
FRIEND THREE
AGENT ONE
AGENT TWO
AGENT THREE
MCIKI RAKE
SHANIE
MAURIE
GLENDA
BILL
SHARON
AUDIENCE ONE
AUDIENCE TWO

CYNTHIA FERGUSON STANDS ALONE ON THE STAGE IN A SPOTLIGHT STARING OUT AT THE AUDIENCE.

CYNTHIA: Hello everyone. First of all I'd like to say just how thrilled I am to be here with you all. The attention you have given me is quite overwhelming but I want you all to know I love each and every one of you and I do appreciate your interest. I won't say it's been an easy road that has brought me to fame but right now I can tell you that I think it has been worth every battle. As I stand here in front of the eyes of the world I hope it is an inspiration to every young person with dreams. Now a lot of you have been asking me recently - just who is the real Cynthia Ferguson? Where did she come from? How did she suddenly find herself in the spotlight? Well my adoring public - I think it only fair that at this stage of my career it is time to share with you all a little bit of my story.

MOTHER AND FATHER ARE IN A TABLEAU WITH RELATIVES ALL AROUND. THE PICTURE SUDDENLY COMES TO LIFE.

MOTHER: Oh I think it's time.

FATHER: Where is our little treasure? Is she ready yet?

MOTHER: We don't want to rush you Cindy darling but everyone out here is waiting.

COUSIN ONE: ASIDE. Here we go again. I can't believe how every family gathering ends up being hijacked by Marj and Harold staging a concert for little Cynthia. It's not as if she's any good.

COUSIN TWO: ASIDE. I know. It's not fair on the poor little girl either. She's going to grow up thinking she's got some special talent and when she realises it's not the truth it'll be horrible for her.

MOTHER: Shhhh you two over there. You know our little angel won't start until she has everyone's attention.

FATHER: Alright then everyone. It's time now to introduce our own little star of the future Cynthia Ferguson.

CYNTHIA COMES INTO THE PICTURE.

CYNTHIA: Thank you, thank you, thank you. And today for you all I am going to do one of my favourite songs. PRESENTS AN EXCRUCIATING VERSION OF POPULAR SONG. THE FAMILY WATCHES AND POLITELY APPLAUDS.

COUSIN ONE: Oh performing is definitely in her blood.

COUSIN TWO: Yes she was born for the stage.

COUSIN ONE: You must be very proud of her.

MOTHER: Yes she is good isn't she.

FATHER: Right from the moment she was born we knew we had a star on our hands.

CYNTHIA: And now I have some more for you. I know every song from Grease and I am going to do them now for you and play every part. Please make yourselves comfortable.

COUSIN ONE: Oh goody.

COUSIN TWO: Lucky us.

MOTHER: I'll make sure you're not disturbed dear. Harold go and take the phone off the hook.

FATHER: Don't start till I get back honey. I don't want to miss a moment of this. CYNTHIA STEPS OUT OF THE SCENE.

CYNTHIA: So you see, I was fortunate to have a real head start in my career thanks to my wonderful, supportive parents. In fact I'd like to say hello to them now because I know that they'll be watching. SHE WAVES. Now of course show business is a very competitive industry and I found that out at a really early stage of my career, right back when I was still at school.

SCHOOL FRIENDS ARE ALL TALKING.

FRIEND ONE: Have you seen Cynthia lately? She is so obsessed about the school play I think she needs therapy.

FRIEND TWO: Tell me about it. She keeps on going on about it as if there was nothing else in the world.

FRIEND THREE: And she just can't get over how Ann got the lead role instead of her. I mean I don't want to be the one to tell her but it's obvious why Ann got the lead.

FRIEND ONE: Yeah poor Cynthia. She really has no idea how bad she is has she?

FRIEND TWO: She was so lucky to even get to be understudy for the lead. I think Mr. Shepherd gave her the understudy part just to keep her quiet. I mean Ann is great.

FRIEND THREE: And Cynth, well if she could act, dance or sing she might have a better chance.

FRIEND ONE: Well that's a pretty big if.

FRIEND TWO: She keeps making me go through her lines with her and she is like totally terrible. She overacts so badly.

FRIEND THREE: Never mind. The show starts tomorrow and once it's out of the way maybe she'll get back to normal.

FRIEND ONE: I don't think that there is a normal for Cynthia Ferguson.

FRIEND TWO: Shhh. Here she comes.

CYNTHIA ARRIVES

CYNTHIA: Hi everyone.

FRIEND THREE: Hi Cynthia. Hey what's up? You look totally stoked about something.

CYNTHIA: Well I just heard something really amazing. Of course you all know how Ann Thompson got the lead in the school play.

FRIEND ONE: Like you've talked about anything else for the past eight weeks.

CYNTHIA: Well face it. She should never have got it. I'm so much better than her. She must have been bribing the teachers or something.

FRIEND TWO: I really don't think that's the case Cynth.

CYNTHIA: Yeah whatever. Well guess what happened to Ann Thompson?

ALL: What?

CYNTHIA: She fell down the stairs in the theatre at rehearsal today and broke her leg. She was just taken away in an ambulance.

FRIEND THREE: That's terrible.

FRIEND ONE: Poor Ann.

FRIEND TWO: How did it happen?

CYNTHIA: Hey come on now. Whose side are you on? She was a total amateur anyway and it serves her right for thinking that she was better than everybody else.

FRIEND THREE: But what happened?

CYNTHIA: No-one knows for sure because no-one was there when it happened. She was just found in a crumpled mess at the bottom of the stairs with her leg behind her ear. Typical Ann though, looking for someone to blame for the fact that she is a clumsy cow. She was saying that someone came up behind her and pushed her. Like as if. Who would do something like that?

FRIEND ONE: Yeah.

FRIEND TWO: As if.

FRIEND THREE: Just an accident.

CYNTHIA: Well lucky for the school I know the part backwards. Now I'll be able to do the lead and the show will be a huge hit.

FRIEND ONE: Yeah.

FRIEND TWO: Lucky.

FRIEND THREE: That's great.

CYNTHIA: Anyway girls I better go and start rehearsing again. Can't keep my audience waiting. SHE EXITS.

FRIEND ONE: What do you reckon?

FRIEND TWO: Surely she wouldn't.

FRIEND THREE: I don't even want to know. THEY FREEZE.

CYNTHIA: Sometimes good fortune smiled on me but most times I had to work hard like every other aspiring star. Once school was finished it was the endless round of agents and casting companies that I had to front up to, trying to find the one that would recognise my special qualities as a performer.
THREE AGENTS ARE LINED UP ACROSS THE STAGE.

AGENT ONE: Look Sandra...

CYNTHIA: It's Cynthia. Cynthia Ferguson.

AGENT ONE: Whatever. The fact is that there isn't really any work for umm what you have to offer. I'm sorry but my advice is to not waste your time. I'm sure you can get a nice job at McDonald's or something.

CYNTHIA: No you haven't given me a chance. Listen if you could just organise a few auditions I know that I can get a role in something. I'm a sure fire star of the future.

AGENT ONE: You want to know how many sure fire stars of the future I meet every day? Sorry but I'm a busy person. Try a few more acting lessons, think about some serious plastic surgery and think about coming back in about five years.

CYNTHIA: You'll be sorry. You'll regret this.

AGENT ONE: Now where have I heard that one before? Don't call us and we won't call you. CYNTHIA MOVES ON TO AGENT TWO.

AGENT TWO: Sorry honey but there's nothing for you in this agency.

CYNTHIA: But you haven't even heard me sing. My mother says I could be the next Celine Dion.

AGENT TWO: Honey one Celine Dion is more than enough already.

CYNTHIA: But I dance as well.

AGENT TWO: Come back next decade when things might have picked up. CYNTHIA GOES TO AGENT THREE.

CYNTHIA: Hello my name is Cynthia Ferguson.

AGENT THREE: Next.

CYNTHIA: But you don't even know...

AGENT THREE: Next!!!! CYNTHIA MOVES DOWNSTAGE.

CYNTHIA: It was a very difficult time for me. Despite all the encouragement I got from my family and friends it seemed that getting my first break into the world of professional show business was going to be harder than I imagined. I admit that there were times that I even became a little bit dismayed. Sometimes I even found it hard to move out of the house and I took to watching daytime television. But strangely enough that proved to be a total inspiration for me thanks to one particular program that I wouldn't miss.

VOICEOVER: And now ladies and gentlemen I'd like you to put your hands together for daytime television's talk show queen Miss Micki Rake.

ENTER MICKI.

MICKI: Hi studio audience and everyone watching at home. My name's Micki Rake and, as always, I am here to bring to you issues that some of you may think strange but surprisingly affect us all. And today's program we are dealing with an increasingly common problem. The title of today's show is 'You Turned My Boyfriend Into A Piece of Furniture'. Now first of all I'd like you all to welcome Shanie. ENTER SHANIE. Now Shanie you have said that you and your boyfriend Maurie were well on your way to making a long term commitment when he was called away on a business trip to Perth. And when he came back, he was no longer the person you had fallen in love with because thanks to the intervention of a doctor who is known only as Pip, Maurie had undergone a change while he was away and come back as a piece of comfortable furniture. Would you like to tell us a little bit about your experience?

SHANIE: Well yes Micki. Maurie and I had been living together for about seven months then listen to this. About two months ago he told me that he had to go away to Perth to attend a business conference for a few days. A few days! Well a few days was all he needed to shock me because I might have waved goodbye to my man but what got off the plane a few days later was a bean bag Micki. A bean bag!! And then Maurie told me that it was over between us because my curtains didn't match his upholstery.

MICKI: And you say you had no idea about this change before he left.

SHANIE: No, none at all. Oh I used to notice when at every party we went to he would put a lampshade on his head but I just thought he was being a joker. But nothing could have prepared me for what took place.

MICKI: Well I can understand that it must have been a shock but as you know there are always two sides to every story. And now it's time to bring out the person at the centre of this fuss. Come on out! ENTER MAURIE:

MAURIE: Hey Micki darlin'. Hi Shanie.

MICKI: Well the first thing I've got to say is you do look well upholstered.

MAURIE: Thanks Micki. It's so nice when someone notices when you take pride in your appearance.

SHANIE: But what are you encouraging this person for. I had plans to marry this...this...this...

MAURIE: Go on say it Shanie. You had plans to marry this beanbag.

MICKI: I have to say he does appear to be very comfortable with himself.

SHANIE: Oh but he looked much better before, trust me.

MICKI: Well Shanie, is there anything to want to say to Maurie now in front of our audience.

SHANIE: Ok well here is the question I want answered. Why? Why? Why?

MAURIE: Shanie sweetheart you know what your problem is? You took the whole thing too personally. It had nothing to do with you. I just felt much more myself this way.

SHANIE: But you could have told me before. And oh I've tried to understand Micki I have tried. We've even gone out together since the change, trying to find out where our relationship is at. But do you know what happens. Every time we go to a club people come up and just want to take over – invite him back to their place to watch a movie or something like that.

MICKI: Is this true Maurie?

MAURIE: Well yes but I have to say it's nice to be treated with respect and for people to appreciate my special qualities. I may be a bean bag now but that doesn't make me a doormat.

SHANIE: Oh you are fooling yourself big time if you think that. You might think you look alright now but what happens when you get drinks spilled on you or someone let's their smelly dog sit on you. How are you going to feel when you are covered in dog hair hey?

MICKI: Hey now settle down please – both of you. Perhaps it's time now to take some feedback from the studio audience. Yes over there with your hand up.

AUDIENCE MEMBER ONE: Hi Micki. I'd just like to say to Shanie 'You go girl!'

MICKI: Thanks for that. Is there another comment over there?

AUDIENCE MEMBER TWO: Just a question for Shanie. If you cared so much for him before the change have you considered changing yourself for the new Maurie rather than wanting to change him back to the way he used to be? I know a good upholsterer who might be able to help you with that.

CYNTHIA TURNS THE TELEVISION OFF.

CYNTHIA: And that was when the idea hit me. This was the way that I was going to be noticed and get my break into show business. I would be a guest on Micki Rake and when people saw how good I looked on television the offers would fly in. So I rang up the producers and found out that they were looking for guests on a program going to air called 'Neighbours From Hell'. Well it took me no time to convince them that my neighbours were the worst in the world, even if I had to bend the truth a little bit, and so it was that I was invited to be a guest on the Micki Rake Show. My career was about to be launched.

THE GUESTS ARE WAITING TO GO ON.

SHARON: Well this is exciting. I've never been on television before.

BILL: I can't believe you talked me into doing this Sharon. The things I do for a bet.

SHARON: Oh it'll be fun and besides we do get paid for this appearance you know.

GLENDA: Well that's the only reason I'm doing it. It seemed an easy way to pick up a bit of cash. TO CYNTHIA. What are you doing on the show love?

CYNTHIA: It's my turn to be discovered. This will give my public the chance to see me.

GLENDA: Yeah, whatever.

SHARON: Shhh. It's about to start.

VOICEOVER: And now ladies and gentlemen, I'd like you to put your hands together for daytime television's talk show queen Miss Micki Rake.

ENTER MICKI.

MICKI: Hi studio audience and everyone at home. Today we are going to be looking at a topic that I know many of you can relate to. Today's topic is 'Neighbours From Hell'. We have quite a few guests lined up to join us today so let's bring them all in. ENTER THE GUESTS. Now as you know when you move into your home one of the things that you hope for is nice neighbours, but sometimes things can go horribly wrong. These people all claim that their lives are a misery because of what their neighbours get up to. Now Glenda, you have got a real problem with the people next door. Would you like to share that with us?

GLENDA: I most certainly would. My neighbour keeps on sneaking over our back fence and putting clothes on my clothesline.

MICKI: Goodness, that's a bit unusual. It would be bad if your neighbour was stealing your clothes from your clothesline but what is so bad about them putting clothes on your clothesline?

GLENDA: The fact is she has the worst taste in clothes. Can you imagine how bad it is to go outside and see ugly clothes hanging on the line? What happens if someone else sees them and thinks they're mine?

MICKI: Oh I can see how that would be a problem.

GLENDA: And it gets worse. She doesn't only put her clothes on my line. She puts her husband's clothes on as well. I was having a friend over for lunch last week and what do you think she saw when she looked into my back yard? A pair of extra large sized y-fronts hanging there. They looked like a sail from a yacht. How was I meant to explain that they weren't mine? She probably thinks that I am sleeping with some fat old man now.

CYNTHIA: You think that's bad. My neighbour...

MICKI: Thanks but we'll get back to you later. Well Glenda perhaps we'll just ask the studio audience if they have anything to say?

AUDIENCE ONE: Thanks Micki. Glenda, all I want to say to you is 'you go girl'.

MICKI: Thanks. Now you over there?

AUDIENCE TWO: If I was you honey I'd throw mud all over her clothes any time they appeared on your line. That ought to stop her doing it.

MICKI: Well it seems the audience wants you to fight back Glenda. Well good luck with the fight. Now we'll move on to our next guest...

CYNTHIA: Yes Micki, my neighbour, oh let me tell you...

MICKI: Our next guest is Sharon who is very distressed by what has been happening next door. Sharon, would you like to share that with the audience and the people at home.

SHARON: I most certainly would. My neighbour is running a brothel for gold fish in his house.

MICKI: Could you tell us more about it?

SHARON: Well I was suspicious when I used to see all these fish tanks being delivered and then I noticed late at night people coming in with their goldfish and leaving them there sometimes for an hour or two, sometimes overnight. When I went and asked him what was going on he said to mind my own business. But if it is going on next door and disturbing the neighbourhood it IS my business.

MICKI: Well you are obviously very distressed by this. But now I'd like to hear the other side of this story and we have your neighbour here with us. Bill, would you like to tell us what's going on in your house.

BILL: Well first I'd like to say that what goes on in my house is my business and there is nothing worse than a nosey neighbour sneaking around trying to look through your windows late at night.

CYNTHIA: Oh yes there is. My neighbour....

MICKI: Yes, yes we'll get to you. Go on Bill.

BILL: Well the truth is that I do have lots of fish tanks. And people do bring their fish over late at night.

SHARON: See he admits it.

BILL: Yes Micki but I own an aquarium. I use my house as a quiet place for breeding goldfish for my shop.

SHARON: Oh my Lord. See he even talks about it on national television.

MICKI: But it hardly seems like a problem to me Sharon.

SHARON: Not a problem. He's breeding goldfish next door. You know what that means? Goldfish are having sex there, all night. Horrible little fishy orgies. It's disgusting.

MICKI: Well we might throw over to the studio audience now.

AUDIENCE ONE: Sharon, all I want to say to you is, 'you go girl'.

MICKI: Thanks for that. Now over there with your hand up.

AUDIENCE TWO: I want to say to Bill that my pet goldfish Terence is pretty lonely and can I bring him around for a visit?

BILL: Any time.

MICKI: Thanks audience. Well our last Guest Cynthia has a problem with her neighbour too.

CYNTHIA: That's right Micki.

MICKI: But unfortunately we have run out of time for today's program so we'll have to leave it there.

CYNTHIA: What?!!!!

MICKI: We'll see you tomorrow when we will be discussing the topic My Grandmother Needs A Makeover.

CYNTHIA: But what about me. Let me speak.

MICKI: Thanks again for coming and...

CYNTHIA: No. NO! You can't do this to me.

MICKI: I'm sorry but we're out of time...

CYNTHIA: Turn the cameras on. It's my turn now.

MICKI: Listen you fruitcake will you just go?

CYNTHIA: I won't let you do this. This was my big chance. I'm not going to let you ruin it. SHE PULLS OUT A KNIFE. Turn the cameras on.

MICKI: Someone get this lunatic out of here.

CYNTHIA: Not before I get on television. SHE JUMPS AT MICKI AND STABS HER. PEOPLE RUSH IN FROM EVERYWHERE TO DRAG HER AWAY. THE SCENE FREEZES AND CYNTHIA GOES BACK TO HER AREA.

CYNTHIA: So you see that was how it happened. I'd like to thank you all for coming to my press conference. I'd like to stay and talk to you some more but the trial is beginning in a few moments and I have to make sure I look alright. But don't worry. I'll be back for you. I know that the world wants more of Cynthia Ferguson and I'm not going to disappoint them. Thank you and good night.

THE END

THE GREAT PRETENDER

CHARACTERS
PUSSY SWINTON
FLUFFY HANDCOCK
BIMBO DE BOOM BOOM
PARIS PENZANCE
RUBY BANG BANG
LEATHER CRACKIT
IVANA GROPE
FATIMA WHIPLASH
SALLY

THE PLAY OPENS WITH AN EXCITING GLAMOROUS MUSICAL PRESENTATION OF A TRULY FABULOUS SONG.

VOICEOVER: So Ladies and Gentlemen that's all we have for you tonight from the Boom Boom Room so let's give a big hand once again for the boys that bring joy whenever they slip into their stilettos. Pussy Swinton. Fluffy Handcock. Bimbo de Boom-boom. Paris Penzance. Ruby Bangbang. Leather Crackit. Ivana Grope and the lovely Fatima Whiplash.

THE 'GIRLS' COME OUT AS THEY ARE INTRODUCED AND FORM A GORGEOUS TABLEAU WHICH THEY HOLD TILL THE LIGHTS DIM.

PUSSY: Oh my Lord I'm glad that's over for the night.

FLUFFY: You're glad. If I don't get out of these shoes soon my feet will just die.

BIMBO: Well serves you right for squeezing into size sevens when everyone knows your feet are so much bigger than that.

FLUFFY: Ooh they are not. How dare you.

PARIS: Don't listen to him Fluffy love. He's just jealous cause he wanted those stilettos out of wardrobe that you got.

RUBY: Well I can't believe I'm saying this but I can't wait to get out of this frock and into something more comfortable.

LEATHER: Me too. It's been a long night boys.

IVANA: Well guess we better get the makeup off and get ready for home.

FATIMA: Yes that's right. Where's Sally I wonder? She's never around when you need her.

PUSSY: Oh she can be a lazy little minx.

FLUFFY: She's like that because she's jealous you know. Poor little plain creature that she is.

LEATHER: Yes surrounded by all this glamour. She's the only girl and she's the one without a single nice frock.

IVANA: Poor love. She can't help it if she hasn't got our sense of style.

BIMBO: Well she has a job to do and she's not doing it. CALLS Sally. Sally where are you? ENTER SALLY.

SALLY: Sorry. I was busy sweeping up the glitter on the stage.

PUSSY: Well honey that can wait. You're meant to be helping us now. Can you hang up my boa darl. It's starting to shed feathers everywhere.

FLUFFY: I know Pussy. You've been leaving tell-tale feathers everywhere.

PUSSY: And what is that supposed to mean?

FLUFFY: Oh nothing. Don't get your jock strap in a twist.

FATIMA: Sally love. Can you please help me with the eyelashes. I need some help getting them off without bending them.

IVANA: You need to use a stronger mascara mate.

FATIMA: Oh I know but you don't want one that sets like concrete so you break your own eyelashes off.

IVANA: True, true.

PARIS: Have you tried this new Long Lash mascara. It's great.

FATIMA: Good old Paris. Always seems to have the information on the latest cosmetics.

PARIS: Well it's just my....sister knows an awful lot about make up that's all.

LEATHER: I didn't know you had a sister? I thought you said you only had two brothers.

PARIS: Did I? You must have heard wrong.

BIMBO: Well who cares. Your sister has been a Godsend to me. That new foundation you recommended is just terrific.

IVANA: I have never had a sister. Just as well we would have ended up fighting over who got to wear what frock on the weekend. THEY ALL GIGGLE.

SALLY: Speaking of frocks, listen guys. Could you please make sure you leave your frocks on the proper hangers. It's been really difficult keeping things organised in wardrobe lately because you keep getting them mixed up.

RUBY: Oh don't be such a fusspot Sally love.

IVANA: Oh be quiet Ruby. Sally's only doing her job. It can't be easy looking after all us guys night after night.

RUBY: Oh I was only teasing. So tell me Sally. Have you found yourself a man yet? It seems dreadful that a young thing like you, even if you have had a glamour bypass, should not have some nice young accountant or something.

SALLY: No. No-one special.

FLUFFY: Well I might be able to send you one of my cast offs if you're looking love.

SALLY: No thanks. I don't think any or your cast offs would be interested in me.

FLUFFY: Oh you'd be surprised.

PUSSY: Honey any of your cast offs would be so worn out they wouldn't be good for anything.

FLUFFY: Oh how dare you!

PUSSY: Just teasing. Friends?

FLUFFY: Of course. Kissy kissy. THEY KISS EACH OTHER ON THE CHEEK.

FATIMA: Hey has anyone got any cotton wool balls. I'm all out.

IVANA: There's another pack in my bag if you want to go and get it.

FATIMA: Thanks hon. SHE EXITS.

IVANA: Have you all heard about Fatima?

RUBY: No. What's the goss?

IVANA: Well you know how hopeless he is with the steps in the new number. I overheard the boss saying that if he doesn't get his act together he'll be dropped from the show.

PARIS: Funny you should say that. I heard something similar about you Ivana.

IVANA: What do you mean?

PARIS: Barry from lighting said that. I'm only repeating what I heard.

PUSSY: Well fellas this is as good a time as any to tell you what I heard from Kevin the sound man. He said that they are going to have a major cutback and that three or four of us might be out of a job by the end of the week. VARIOUS EXCLAMATIONS

OF OUTRAGE. Look don't yell at me. I'm only repeating what I have heard.

BIMBO: Sally have you heard anything about this?

SALLY: I might have heard something. Nothing definite. They were just saying that some of the patrons lately haven't been all that impressed because they don't think you make convincing enough women when you are on stage.

PUSSY: Outrageous!

FLUFFY: Impossible!

LEATHER: Who said that?

SALLY: So they are just reviewing the show this week and they'll make some decisions soon.

FATIMA: Oh no. This is terrible. I don't want to lose my job.

RUBY: I love this job. Where else am I going to get this kind of glamour and excitement?

PARIS: Well I'm sure I've got nothing to worry about. Paris Penzance is the queen of glamour. They won't sack me.

BIMBO: Paris darl we're all queens of one kind or another here. I don't think anyone is safe.

SALLY: Well fellas I wouldn't worry about it at the moment. Who knows what will be happening at the end of the week?

RUBY: Oh I need something to settle me down after all that bad news. Sally be a love and get me a peppermint tea will you.
THE OTHERS ALL PUT IN ORDERS AS WELL.

SALLY: Alright. I'll be right back. SHE EXITS. FATIMA RE-ENTERS.

FATIMA: Ivana. That was your bag in the corner wasn't it? The blue one?

IVANA: Yes, blue to match my nails. Did you get the cotton balls?

FATIMA: I got something more interesting than cotton balls. Care to explain these? HOLDS OUT A DISPOSABLE NAPPY AND A BOTTLE.

IVANA: Where did you get them?

FATIMA: They were in your bag.

LEATHER: What are you doing with things like THAT in your bag?

IVANA: Umm they must belong to my... sister. She has a little boy about one year old. I sometimes babysit. That's where they're from.

PUSSY: You said that you didn't have a sister before Ivana.

FLUFFY: Got you there Ivana. What's going on? What are you trying to hide?

IVANA: I'm not trying to hide anything.

FATIMA: Then what are you doing with a nappy and a bottle in your bag. If I looked further I wonder what else I would have found.

IVANA: You might have found my fist in your face. How dare you go snooping through my things.

FATIMA: I was only looking for the cotton balls.

BIMBO: So what's the story mate? Don't tell me you have a wife and baby tucked away somewhere that you've been keeping a secret from us.

IVANA: I think you should all just mind your own business.

PARIS: Why when this is so much more interesting. I wonder how the boss would feel if he knew one of his boys was keeping a family tucked away.

LEATHER: Perhaps the boss should be told. If heads are going to roll at the end of the week I'm sure the first person they would want to get rid of is one that doesn't tell the truth.

IVANA: I bet if you looked closely everyone here would have their little secrets. I'm not the only one.

PUSSY: Oh really? I'm sure I've got nothing to hide.

FLUFFY: Oh no? What about this you dropped last week. PULLS OUT A BRA.

PUSSY: Where did you get that?

FLUFFY: You dropped it in the carpark. I picked it up but you had already driven off.

PUSSY: It's just part of my costume.

FLUFFY: Come on now Pussy. Since when is target brand underwear part of your costume. Seems a funny thing to be carrying around.

PUSSY: Funny like your Health Care card you mean.

FLUFFY: Health Care card?

PUSSY: Sorry hon but I couldn't help but have a little peek when you left your wallet on the dressing table. I just wanted to have a laugh at your driver's licence. You know how people always look dreadful in their licence photos. I got more of a surprise than I bargained for that's for sure.

FLUFFY: Well if I knew I was in a room full of such sticky noses I would have locked my personal belongings away.

PUSSY: Well I did manage to keep it a secret but I won't any more unless you keep your mouth shut.

LEATHER: Come on fellas settle down.

RUBY: No let them go I'm enjoying this.

LEATHER: As much as you enjoy shopping at Safeway.

RUBY: Excuse me?

LEATHER: I didn't believe it to begin with when I first saw you. I didn't recognise you at first but then I saw you over a few weeks and I suddenly realised that it could only be you. Wouldn't the other fellas like to know what you look like in your day to day clothes.

RUBY: You're making all this up. You're just trying to cause trouble for other people so they get kicked out and you keep your job here.

BIMBO: Yeah that'd be right. It's the only way that you could keep your job here. You are the worst dancer in the whole group. And as for that bust of yours. It is the fakest thing I have ever seen. If you are going to use fake boobs try using ones that look like genuine silicone instead of balloons with water in them.

LEATHER: Mate if you are looking for a punch in the face then you're going the right way about it.

RUBY: Don't think I have anything to worry about from you. You probably hit like a girl.

LEATHER: Yeah well rather hit like a girl than have to sit down every time I go to the toilet.

PARIS: Um fellas. I think we all better calm down.

FATIMA: Shut up you makeup queen. How is it that you are such an expert on make up anyway. That line about your sister - as if anyone believes it. We have had too many sisters that don't exist in this room if you ask me.

PARIS: Yeah well no amount of makeup can save that face of yours buddy.

BIMBO: I've had it. I'm getting out of here right now. I don't want to waste any more time with any of you tonight. I don't know what's going on here but I think it would be better for everyone if we all just shut up mind our own business and go home.

PUSSY: Better for you in particular Bimbo de Boom-boom. Or should I say Miss Fitzgerald.

BIMBO: What are you talking about? I'm out of here.

PUSSY: You're not going anywhere. I've seen you during the week. I know what you do during the day. And you thought you were so clever.

FLUFFY: You don't mean....

PUSSY: Yes fellas. Bimbo de Boom-boom by night, but by day that person is Miss Fitzgerald, local kindergarten teacher. STUNNED SILENCE.

IVANA: Do you mean to tell me.....

PUSSY: Yes, that person is a woman.

BIMBO: I am not. You liar.

FLUFFY: Don't call my friend a liar you great big fat fake.

BIMBO: How dare you call me fat. CHARGES AT FLUFFY. THEY START TO TUSSLE. THE STRUGGLE ESCALATES UNTIL ALL EIGHT ARE INVOLVED. WIGS FLY. ENTER SALLY.

SALLY: Hey fellas. What is going on here? Stop please. You'll break something.

PARIS: Fellas. Hah that's a joke.

RUBY: Where's my wig?

FATIMA: Oh why bother? Let's face it. The game is up for all of us.

PUSSY: If you had just minded your own business.

FLUFFY: If you hadn't gone snooping in the first place.

PARIS: What's the point? We were all going to get caught out some time.

SALLY: Caught out. What are you all talking about?

IVANA: Open your eyes Sally. Look at us.

PARIS: Sally we're all women.

SALLY: But that's impossible. How can you be? This is a drag revue.

PUSSY: You think we don't know that.

SALLY: But why?

PUSSY: Well I can't speak for the others but I've been trying to get a break into show business for years without success. When I saw the ad asking for female impersonators I thought well it's worth a try.

IVANA: I was stuck at home with a new baby, I was just looking for a bit of excitement in my life.

RUBY: The money's good. It's better than what I get at my part time job as a check out chick.

PARIS: And it seemed a great way to keep up my orders with Avon and much easier than going door to door. You lot have bought more in the past three months than I sell in a year.

RUBY: But I guess the game is up.

LEATHER: Yeah the boss won't want any of us when he finds out will he?

SALLY: Well he doesn't need to find out does he?

PUSSY: What do you mean?

SALLY: Well I think everyone has their little secrets. Why don't you just pack up and go home and pretend this little incident never happened. I can keep a secret.

FLUFFY: Sally you're a doll.

PARIS: Thanks Sally. You're great.

SALLY: It's alright. Look I'll see you all tomorrow night. SHE EXITS.

BIMBO: What a sweetheart.

RUBY: Yeah she's a life saver.

FATIMA: Well girls. I am totally wiped out after this excitement. Time to go home. SHE STANDS TO EXIT.

IVANA: Wait. You forgot your bag.

FATIMA: It's not my bag.

RUBY: I think it belongs to Sally.

IVANA: Sally? Hmmm HAS A QUICK LOOK IN THE BAG. Are you sure this is Sally's bag.

RUBY: I saw her bring it in.

IVANA: Hmmm.. Then I wonder why she is carrying around an electric shaver.

THE END

CHRISTMAS TURKEY

CHARACTERS
MUM
DAD
BRETT
BARBIE
BILLY
BEN
BOB
BETTY
GRANDMA
GRANDPA

SETTING: THE FAMILY LIVING ROOM ON CHRISTMAS MORNING. DAD IS TIDYING UP THE ROOM WHEN MUM ENTERS.

MUM: John. The turkey's not in the fridge. Where did you leave it?

DAD: I didn't leave it anywhere dear. I haven't touched the turkey.

MUM: But where did you put it when I told you to take it out of the freezer yesterday.

DAD: You didn't tell me to do anything with the turkey.

MUM: Of course I did. Yesterday afternoon, before we went to Grandma's for the Christmas party.

DAD: Well I didn't hear you then. We were in a bit of a hurry.

MUM: But if you didn't get it out of the freezer then... RUSHING OUT, THEN FROM OFFSTAGE. Oh, oh no. THE CHILDREN COME RUSHING IN.

BILLY: What's wrong with Mum?

BOB: What's happened? MUM COMES BACK.

MUM: The turkey was still in the freezer. It's hard as a rock.

DAD: Can't you just put it in the oven like that?

MUM: No, it won't cook properly. And it says here that it needs twenty four hours to defrost properly. What are we going to do?

BETTY: What time are Grandma and Grandpa coming for lunch?

MUM: In about three hours.

DAD: Well we'd better get to work then. Brett, turn on the heater.

BRETT: But it's the middle of summer. It's going to be thirty four degrees today.

DAD: Don't argue. We've got to get this turkey defrosted. Turn the heater up to full and get Barbie and Ben to hold the turkey in a towel across the front of the heater. AFTER A BIT OF RUSHING AROUND, THE TURKEY IS IN ITS TOWEL HAMMOCK IN FRONT OF THE HEATER.

BEN: Mum. Dad. I'm hot.

BARBIE: Me too.

DAD: Alright then. Betty and Brett. Hold the turkey for your brother and sister while they change into their bathers. Billy. Bob. You go and get a couple of fans to help keep your brother and sister cool while they defrost the turkey.

BILLY: But won't that keep the turkey cool as well?

DAD: Oh. I hadn't thought of that. Alright then. Get them a bucket of cold water each to stand in. WHILE THEY ARE DOING THAT BARBIE AND BEN RETURN.

BARBIE: Has it defrosted any yet?

BETTY: Don't be silly. It's still hard as a rock.

BRETT: This doesn't seem to be doing much good Dad.

MUM: I know. I'll get the hair dryer onto it. That'll get things started. Barbie. You go and get the hair dryer out of the bathroom. BILLY AND BOB RETURN.

BOB: Where will we put these?

DAD: Oh we don't need them now. Just put them out of the way. THEY PUT THE BUCKET DOWN. BARBIE RUNS IN WITH THE HAIR DRYER AND STEPS IN THE BUCKET.

BARBIE: Help. My foot's stuck.

DAD: Ben. Get the bucket off Barbie's foot. Bob. Grab the hair dryer and get it turned onto the turkey.

MUM: Oh we're never going to get it defrosted in time.

DAD: Are you sure it won't fit into the microwave love?

MUM: It's twice as big as our microwave. If you hadn't been such a cheapskate when you brought it...

DAD: Well if I didn't have to give the kids so much pocket money I might have been able to afford a bigger microwave.

BILLY: Don't blame us.

BETTY: Yeah. We don't get as much pocket money as most kids any way.

MUM: This is no time to discuss pocket money. Bob, is the hair dryer making any difference?

BOB: Not so far Mum.

BARBIE: Does the local chicken shop sell turkey?

BRETT: Don't be silly. They'd be sold out by now.

BEN: I don't think the chicken shop would be open at 9.30 a.m. on Christmas Day anyway.

MUM: Oh, if only we could fit it into the microwave. Then we could defrost it.

DAD: Maybe there is a way to fit it into the microwave. Ben, Billy. Go out to the garage and fetch the chainsaw.

BETTY: What are you going to do Dad?

DAD: Well if the whole turkey doesn't fit into the microwave, I'll saw it in half and we can defrost it a half at a time.

MUM: You can't do that. How will the stuffing stay in?

DAD: You'll just have to wrap each half in foil. Off you go boys.

BOB: Do I have to keep on hair drying the turkey?

DAD: You might as well. Every little bit helps.

MUM: Well, while your Father is chain-sawing the turkey, why don't the rest of you help me get started on the vegies. Brett, Barbie. Why don't you peel the potatoes? Betty, you can do the carrots.

DAD: Bob, you'd better bring the turkey into the laundry. I don't think it's a good idea to use the chainsaw in the living room.

BOB: Okay Dad. THE ROOM CLEARS EXCEPT FOR MUM, WHO BEGINS TO SING NERVOUSLY TO CHEER HERSELF UP.

MUM: SINGING: Deck the halls with boughs of holly
Fa la la la la la la la la
Tis the season to be jolly, Fa la la la
THE SOUND OF A CHAINSAW IS HEARD BUT IT SUDDEN CRUNCHES TO A HALT.

DAD: OFFSTAGE. Oh no! HE ENTERS. The chainsaw just broke. It's as if the turkey was made of stone.

MUM: Well there's only one thing for it. We're going to have to just shove it in the oven, turn the oven up to high and hope for the best. I don't think that Christmas can stand much more of this.

DAD: Well, you're the boss. Let's go and get everything else organized. THEY EXIT. A FEW MOMENTS OF SOME

CHRISTMAS MUSIC IS PLAYED TO SUGGEST THE PASSAGE OF A FEW HOURS. THE DOOR BELL RINGS. ENTER BILLY, IN NICE CLOTHES. HE ANSWERS THE DOOR.

BILLY: Oh Hi Grandma. Hi Grandpa. Come on in. ENTER GRANDMA AND GRANDPA. BILLY CALLS. Hey everyone. Grandma and Grandpa are here. THE FAMILY ENTERS ONE AT A TIME, GREETING THEIR GRANDPARENTS. MUM AND DAD ARE THE LAST TO ENTER.

MUM: Hello Mum. Hi Dad. Merry Christmas.

DAD: Merry Christmas.

GRANDMA: Merry Christmas darling. Goodness. It's hot in the house?

DAD: Do you think so? I'll turn the air conditioner on.

BOB: I know why it's so hot Grandma. It's because...

MUM: GRABBING HIM AND COVERING HIS MOUTH. It's because everyone is so excited about Christmas I suppose. Come and sit down. EVERYONE SETTLES THEMSELVES IN THE LOUNGE ROOM.

GRANDPA: Well I must say I'm looking forward to lunch. There's nothing like good old Christmas turkey roast even on a hot day.

GRANDMA: That's right. We haven't had a big breakfast so we've got plenty of room for lunch.

BARBIE: Well you've got a bit of a wait ahead of you because...

DAD: ...because we wanted to give your present to you first, isn't that right everyone.

GRANDMA: But dear, we usually wait until after lunch to give out the presents.

DAD: Well, we thought that we'd enjoy our meal more if we weren't wondering what presents we were getting while we were eating.

GRANDMA: Well if that's the way you want to do things, how about you kids coming out to the car with your Grandfather and me to help bring the presents in.

BEN: Sure thing. Come on everyone. GRANDMA, GRANDPA AND THE KIDS EXIT.

MUM: Whew. That was close. You know how much Mum and Dad love their Christmas turkey.

DAD: How is it going? It's been in the oven at top temperature for three hours. Is it close to being cooked?

MUM: Well the last time I looked it seemed to getting softer and it was certainly going brown, although it's hard to tell whether it's cooking in the middle or not.

DAD: Well I guess we can just eat the outside bits. BILLY COMES RUNNING IN.

BILLY: Mum. Dad. There's a whole lot of smoke coming out of the kitchen window.

MUM: Oh no. The turkey. SHE RUNS INTO THE KITCHEN AS THE REST OF THE FAMILY COMES THROUGH THE DOOR.

GRANDPA: Quick. It looks like your kitchen's on fire.

DAD: It's alright. Don't panic. We've got everything under control. Everyone just take a seat and calm down. MUM ENTERS WITH A CHARCOAL VERSION OF A TURKEY.

GRANDMA: Good heavens dear. What's that?

MUM: It's – nothing to worry about.

GRANDPA: What do you mean nothing to worry about. It looks like something that has been cremated.

DAD: Well yes. I guess there's something we should tell you. There's no sense in hiding it.

MUM: Yes….we've… decided to become vegetarians this year. Dinner will be ready in ten minutes. SHE RUNS OUT.

THE END

OTHER TITLES AVAILABLE FROM
ORiGiN™ THEATRICAL

CONNECTED
Craig Christie

CONNECTED explores the dangers and consequences of the interface between life and the online world in a story that resonates throughout schools and households everywhere.

Emma arrives at a new school and runs the gauntlet of finding out about friendship groups and how the game is played in this new setting. Meanwhile Dylan's social awkwardness means he is spending more and more time on his computer locked away in his room. When Emma finds herself the object of unwanted attention of the school jock Michael, his ex girlfriend Kate uses any means available to put the new girl in her place. The entire situation takes a turn towards the sinister as their online worlds collides with their lives in a way over which they ultimately have no control and which threatens to have the most disastrous consequences.

"The pace was fast moving and we witnessed the rapid snowballing effect born from the use of modern technology mixed with tricks, lies and deceit. 'Connected' is a perfect platform for young actors to perform to their utmost strengths, the work is vocally demanding and offers the best of opportunities for great acting.
– Scott Jarrett. Whakatane, New Zealand

Cast: 2 Male & 2 Female

www.origintheatrical.com.au

OTHER TITLES AVAILABLE FROM
ORiGiN™ THEATRICAL

MILLIE'S WAR
Dorian Mode

Based on historical events, Millie's War is set in the 1980s when a number of women attempted to join official ANZAC Day marches across Canberra to commemorate women raped in war.

Fourteen women were arrested. The following year, again in Canberra, around 250 women attempted to join the tail of the official ANZAC Day march but were stopped by police. The police were acting under a Section 23A of the Traffic Ordinance, a section conveniently gazetted the day before the march.

Approximately 64 people, mainly women, were arrested and charged.

With this dramatic backdrop, Millie's War is set largely in the boardroom of an RSL Club. When the sleepy local branch of this RSL meet with the women in order to dissuade them from upsetting their sacred parade of remembrance, the crotchety president of the RSL Club is appalled to find his own granddaughter is one of the feminists attempting to spoil their day. Tempers soon reach boiling point as each side argues the case for the importance of commemorating victims of war.

Cast: 4 Male & 3 Female

www.origintheatrical.com.au

Printed by Libri Plureos GmbH in Hamburg, Germany